EXCUSE ME, PASTOR, I DON'T WANT YOUR CHURCH!

(New Edition)

Dr. Michael A. Shine, JD, M.B.A, LSSGB.

Gotham Books

30 N Gould St.
Ste. 20820, Sheridan, WY 82801
https://gothambooksinc.com/

Phone: 1 (307) 464-7800

© 2024 *Dr. Michael A. Shine, JD, M.B.A, LSSGB*. All rights reserved.

No part of this book may be reproduced, stored in a retrieval system, or transmitted by any means without the written permission of the author.

Published by Gotham Books (November 22, 2024)

ISBN: 979-8-3305-8409-3 (H)
ISBN: 979-8-3305-8407-9 (P)
ISBN: 979-8-3305-8408-6 (E)

Because of the dynamic nature of the Internet, any web addresses or links contained in this book may have changed since publication and may no longer be valid.

The views expressed in this work are solely those of the author and do not necessarily reflect the views of the publisher, and the publisher hereby disclaims any responsibility for them.

Dedication

This book is respectfully dedicated to all members of the body of Christ and those who struggle with this organism that is called Church! In addition, I am continuing to speak boldly for the voiceless people who have been hurt and are hurting from the ills of pastors in their approach to ministry.

Special Thanks

I would like to render a special thanks to all pastors who have blessed and helped me in ministry. To my current Pastor Anthony Xavier Page, (Face2Face Worship Center, Clinton, MD) and to my late Pastor Clyde Beverly, Sr. (Pastor Emeritus, First Missionary Baptist Church of East Boyles, Birmingham, AL) who also loved me and assisted me in ministry. I cannot forget my loving Shine, and Hardy, family and my late birth father Mose Shine, Jr. and my loving and caring mother, Odessa Shine, who assisted me in getting this book on the market and who is always there for me in whatever venture in ministry God entrusts to my care.

To all of my special friends near and far (I love each of you!) I cannot forget all people who strong with this organism called "Church." I pray this book makes you proud of me.

Love,

Dr. Michael A. Shine, JD,M.B.A, LSSGB

Table of Contents

Dedication iii
Special Thanks iv
Foreword vii
Introduction ix
Chapter 1: What Is the Church? 1
Chapter 2: God's Vision and Not Mine 7
Chapter 3: Did I Get on the "I" Plan or God's Plan? 11
Chapter 4: Don't Punk Out! 13
Chapter 5: All I Want Is to Help Lift Your Arms 18
Chapter 6: Saul: The Distressed and Possessive King 25
Chapter 7: Jealous Leaders Can Cause Division in the Kingdom 29
Chapter 8: Excuse Me Pastor, the Gifts Are from God and Not from You! 34
Chapter 9: Excuse Me Pastor, I Don't Want Your Pulpit…I Have My Own! 40
Chapter 10: Excuse Me Pastor, I Understand That I Am Not the Senior Pastor 47
Chapter 11: Excuse Me Pastor, Are You Intimidated or Jealous? . 54
Chapter 12: Excuse Me Pastor, but You Are Lazy! 63
Chapter 13: Excuse Me Pastor, You Are Immature! 69
Chapter 14: Excuse Me Pastor, Are You on Death Row? ... 80
Chapter 15: Excuse Me Pastor, Are You Suffering from PMS? 91

Chapter 16: Excuse Me Pastor, Are You Addicted to Porn? 114

Chapter 17: Excuse Me Pastor, Do You Want Money or Ministry? 120

Chapter 18: Excuse Me Pastor, I Can't Come to Your Church Because I Am Gay!.. 129

Chapter 19: Excuse Me Pastor, Don't Violate Me! 144

Chapter 20: Excuse Me Pastor, Can You Pray for Me? 149

Chapter 21: Excuse Me Pastor, Don't Hinder My Praise! 156

Chapter 22: Excuse Me Pastor, Do You Really Love Me? 168

Chapter 23: How to Confront Your Pastor 176

Chapter 24: Nine (9) Lies about the Pastoral Title 184

Chapter 25: About the Author 193

Bibliography 195

Foreword

I am honored to write the foreword for this very transparent and Kingdom-challenging book by Dr. Michael A. Shine. God has allowed me to pastor Dr. Michael for several years. I share this because God has allowed me to see the purity of his heart and experience the honor he demonstrates towards senior leadership. Dr. Michael is a man of integrity with a servant's heart. He is not an individual who covets position or titles. His heartbeat is to serve God and His people in the spirit of excellence, with a burden to see believers realize their true identity in Christ.

The book you hold in your hand chronicles the challenges Dr. Michael A. Shine experienced in church and specifically with leadership who focused not on sharing the liberating gospel of Jesus Christ that saves but instead created stumbling blocks preventing people from experiencing the authentic love of Jesus Christ. This manuscript is a clarion call about what happens when leadership stops focusing on establishing the Kingdom of God and instead builds kingdoms unto themselves, seeking to rule and dominate God's people. Dr. Michael calls these institutional strongholds placed upon Christians and church attendees. Through sharing his experience, he further reveals what happens when leadership forces people through religious traditions, manipulation, and intimidation to serve the God of their dreams and not the one and only true God!

"Excuse Me Pastor, I Don't Want Your Church!" deals with real issues and examples of how people, when controlled by power-hungry leaders, can be financially molested and emotionally abused. The reality is that when leadership lacks a shepherd's heart, abuse is inevitable.

If you are ready to deal with the problematic truths Dr. Michael experienced with church leadership, find a quiet spot, grab a coffee or your favorite soft drink, and set aside two hours to read this riveting book. Please understand that this book does not seek to accuse all spiritual leaders; instead, Dr. Michael provides biblical truths on how believers can find common ground to alleviate these maladies in the church.

May you be inspired to pray for all spiritual leaders that they will develop God's heart to shepherd and lead people in a manner that glorifies Him.

Anthony X. Page,

Lead Pastor, Face2Face Worship Center

Clinton, Maryland

Introduction

I have come to realize that church can be the very stage to play out one's inner emotions, talents and abilities. It has now become a place where the synergy of a person's life that was once viewed as a place of healing and restoration is a place where a person's wounds are turned into spiritual cancer. Some may not take the title positively or receive it for maturation, so I do apologize if I do not tickle your emotions. Others may say that I am wrong. However, it is not about me, but about God's Kingdom being magnified. I have come to the realization that some of us are not going to church to hear the Word of the Lord, but some are going to get the next great piece of gossip, or see what brother or sister "all-right" is wearing. This is in total opposition of why Christ died on the cross. Jesus stated, "Upon this rock I will build my church and the gates of hell shall not prevail against it (Matt. 16:18). Jesus is letting us know that the building block of what He has designed the "Church" for is not for fashion, fighting and fussing, but it is a place where the downtrodden and those poor in spirit come and get a spiritual renewal. It is a place where the like-minded and those yet indifferent come to find rest for their souls.

The title of this book arises out of personal experiences that I have seen, experienced and discerned and not what I have heard. I am not talking about the black church only! Excuse me, it happens everywhere. There is only one true *Church* universally though there are many buildings. I may use the word church in reference to the building but, in some cases, I am talking about the body of baptized believers. This is the very essence of why we have so many churches on each corner and no one is coming to be saved. People are being misled, and many of us are at fault. We have gospel musicals, plays, and annual padding pocket days, only to realize that it is not God's purpose for His Church. I see some pastors and preachers turning people away because they do not look like you or me; while we have the fortunate pleasure of coming to a building with cathedral ceilings and crisp white walls, ornate light fixtures only to find out it is all about the pastor and not about ministry…what a tragedy! Where did we get off course? The Church was once the mainstay of every community where all people could come to get help and assistance, but now people's eyes are opened to a different arena.

We see some pastors, bishops, overseers, and church-goers promoting self as a type of God. I know I can write this because I am a minister and I write what is in my heart and also inspired by God. I know Jesus never gave any thought to self-elevation; however, it seems that the modern-day preacher or pastor does not care about God's vision anymore. I have seen the *Church* go without true ministry so that a pastor can get most or all of the money. Thus, no real ministries are carried out. Moreover, some ministers have started ministries without a clear vision from God. It seems that some pastors' only goal is to make their packets fat. They fail to work like the Apostle Paul who was a tent maker and did not care about money alone, but the souls of God's Kingdom. I do understand that we are to take care of pastors and leaders, but not to the point of worshipping them.

I write this book not because I am better than any but for all Christians who may never speak these words aloud. This book is also for those who cannot seem to put into words what they have seen or experienced--for those voiceless individuals whose needs have been neglected. I believe it is not solely the duty of the "world system" to take care of the poor, the widow and the downtrodden. It is the *Church*! Especially, the pastor that does not have clear vision or the wherewithal to carry out Matthew 28: 19-20 (AMP):

"Go then and make disciples of all the nations, baptizing them into the name of the Father and of the Son and of the Holy Spirit, Teaching them to observe everything that I have commanded you, and behold, I am with you all the days (perpetually, uniformly, and on every occasion), to the [very] close and consummation of the age. Amen"

I have been in ministry for twenty plus years and I have experienced pastors and preachers acting like church buildings are their stage and the members are their cast. There is a blatant disconnect of love resulting in apathy and uncompromising disrespect for what God created and allowed us to care for and defend. I know my calling is not to pastor a church at this time in my life. But I do believe that there are some pastors who are intimidated by the gifting of others that are part of the local body (which will be discussed later in this book).

I was told once that I was out of line for correcting a pastor and yet not rebuking an elder when he or she is wrong. But how do you deal with the following Scripture in *Galatians 6: 1-4 (amp)* which states:

"Brethren, if any person is overtaken in misconduct or sin of any sort, you who are spiritual [who are responsive to and controlled by the Spirit] should set him right and restore and reinstate him, without any sense of superiority and with all gentleness, keeping an attentive eye on yourself, lest you should be tempted also. Bear (endure, carry) one another's burdens and troublesome moral faults, and in this way fulfill and observe perfectly the law of Christ (the Messiah) and complete what is lacking [in your obedience to it]. For if any person thinks himself to be somebody [too important to condescend to shoulder another's load] when he is nobody [of superiority except in his own estimation], he deceives and deludes and cheats himself. But let every person carefully scrutinize and examine and test his own conduct and his own work. He can then have the personal satisfaction and joy of doing something commendable [in itself alone] without [resorting to] boastful comparison with his neighbor."

Is the pastor (he or she) not a man (gender neutral) first. Has the pastor not been called to carry out God's mandate to propagate the Gospel and not pimp it?

This book, **"Excuse Me, Pastor! I Don't Want Your Church,"** is birthed out of inspiration and not jealousy. It is my deepest desire that we all gain a better insight regarding what the purpose of "God's Church, His Mission and His vessel" really is. I do believe that many people are not coming to our local buildings because we have been tricked by Satan into thinking that the building is *"The Church."* Some may have also actually believed that the *Church* belongs to a man and not to God Himself. New buildings are built, new programs come and go, and the "hottest" choirs simply become a vapor before our eyes.

The question still remains: are people really getting to know Christ as their personal Savior? This writing will give some insights (not that I am "Holy Ghost Central,") but to further help, correct, elevate, build and not tear down what the title of the book is stating. It is my sincere desire not to desecrate God's Word, His Message or His Messenger, but to be a voice like that of John the Baptist crying in the wilderness. So, Excuse Me, Pastor, I Don't Want Your Church!

Chapter 1

What Is the Church?

I read an article from "Focus on the Family" while preparing this book and I want to include it in this section to really bring home the message that I am conveying. It stated, *"What is the church?" Now that seems like an easy question, the sort of question one might answer in a simple sentence or two. "A church is a building in which Christians meet for worship" is one obvious possibility. "A church is a group of Christians who gather for religious purposes" is another. A critic might say, "A church is a club for insiders and hypocrites."* These quick answers do not take us very far if we want to understand truly what a church ought to be.

You will notice that I moved from the descriptive – what a church is – to its purpose – what a church ought to be. In this section on the church, I am not so much interested in what churches actually are, or in what people think churches are, as I am in *what churches should be*. When I ask the question "What is the church?" I'm wondering about the ideal rather than the factual.

The visible and local church is, of course, the physical church that we see around us and around the world, as well as the members of those churches. The invisible and universal church, however, refers to all believers everywhere. When most people hear the word 'church' they probably think of a building. Maybe it is a fancy building or a simple building where believers gather. But biblically speaking, a church is much more than a building. In fact, some would say that the church is not a building at all, but is all about the people. But what is the church?

The area of theology that seeks to understand all aspects of the church is known as ecclesiology. It is derived from the Greek word *ekklesia* (*The Called Out Ones*) that is, a general term referring to a gathering or assembly. There are a number of aspects to the subject of ecclesiology, but this portion will focus on defining the term 'church,' understanding its nature and purpose, looking at some biblical images of the church and emphasizing church unity on essential truths.

The early Christian church had no buildings, at least not in the sense of what we would consider church buildings today. First century Christians were often persecuted and, as a result, often met in secret, usually in homes. As the influence of Christianity spread, eventually buildings dedicated to worship were established and became what we know today as churches. In this sense, then, the church consists of people not buildings. Fellowship, worship and ministry are all conducted by people, not buildings. Church structures facilitate the role of God's people, but they do not fulfill it.

When speaking of the church, theologians often use terms such as the visible and local church as opposed to the invisible and universal church. The visible and local church is, of course, the physical church building that we see around us and around the world, as well as the members of those churches. The invisible and universal church, however, refers to all believers everywhere and is one church, united in

Christ, not many physical buildings. Everyone in the universal church is a true believer, but such is not necessarily the case with visible and local churches.

Why is it relevant to understand some basic differences between the visible and universal church? One key reason is so that we do not confuse what we sometimes see fallible churches doing with the reality of the universal church. Not only do visible and local churches often host non-believers, but also the believers themselves are imperfect, resulting in challenges and tensions in every visible church.

The church is not a building, but a body of believers with a specific nature and purpose. These biblical roles or ministries of the church are foundational to it. What are these roles? They are many, but key to any church are foundations in worship, edification and evangelism.

Worship is God-centered and Christ-centered. It is not about entertaining Christians with flashy displays or presentations, but about expressing our love by worshiping our Creator. We are to praise and glorify God in worship. As such, every Christian needs to be part of regular fellowship and worship.

Edification is also a role of the church. It involves edifying believers, but also nurturing, building up or helping believers to mature in Christ. To this end, churches are tasked with a variety of ministries such as Bible study, continuing education in related areas, praying for one another, acts of genuine hospitality and more.

Evangelism is also a key role of the church. This means reaching out to a lost world with the Good News about Jesus. Since people often have questions or doubts about Christ and Christianity, knowing the truth and being able to defend it (apologetics) is also part of the role of the church. However, beyond evangelism in the sense of reaching out with the gospel, the church must express compassion and mercy tangibly by helping others. In following Christ's example to love others, the church, too, must seek to make a real difference in the world while not neglecting to share the message of Christ.

If a church fails to fulfill any of these key roles - worship, edification, and evangelism - then the church is not functioning as God intends. Granted, there are times when churches face challenges and struggles to one degree or another, but a healthy church seeks to overcome such challenges in a way that honors God and His intentions for His church.

There are many images of the church in the Bible, but we will mention just three: the church as the Body of Christ, the People of God and the Bride of Christ. Christ is the head of the church (Ephesians 1:10; 4:15) and Christians are the body. "People of God" is another image of the church. God says of the church, "I will be their God, and they will be my people" (2 Corinthians 6:16; Hebrews 8:10 NIV). The church is also referred to as the Bride of Christ (2 Corinthians 11:2; Ephesians 5:32; Revelation 19:7; 21:9), suggestive of a special and sacred family relationship between Christ and the church.

The concept of the visible and local church also touches briefly on the challenges and tensions that sometimes result in churches. Critics point to divisions and disagreements among Christians as evidence of a lack of unity and hence, they claim unity lacks real biblical support undergirding the Christian Church as a whole. Is this a true statement? In some cases Christians do indeed need to admit to shortcomings and at times, un-Christ-like behavior.

But in looking at the bigger picture, the Christian church has always been united on key points of belief such as the reality of a personal, loving God, salvation that is found in Christ through His death and bodily resurrection, human depravity and the need for redemption through Christ and more. This "mere" Christianity or core of unshakable truths has united Christian churches throughout the centuries and continues to do so.

As one writer once shared, *"In spite of all the unfortunate differences between Christians, what we agree on is still something pretty big and pretty solid: big enough to blow any of us sky-high if it happens to be true. And if it's true, it's quite ridiculous to put off doing anything about it simply because Christians don't fully agree among themselves."* In other words, when it comes to the essentials or primary matters, Christians are united, but when it comes to non-essentials or secondary matters, there is room for some disagreement. This disagreement, however, does not change the unity based on the foundations of Christianity, such as the person of Christ and His role in human redemption.

Again, the Christian church is not a building, but a body of believers united in Christ. Its role is to worship God, nurture and edify and reach out to a suffering world with the saving message of the gospel as well as the practical compassion and mercy exemplified in Christ. To this end, ecclesiology is not some ivory-tower, academic discipline removed from the reality of daily life. Instead, learning more about the church helps us make a real difference in the world, not just temporally, but for all eternity.

Chapter 2

God's Vision and Not Mine

<u>Habakkuk 2:2</u>

Vision gives clarity and insight to unclear things! It causes the unlearned to be deemed learned. I found myself in a situation in which I was forced to deal with a pastor who started a local ministry and he wanted to use a leadership team to write a vision statement. I immediately questioned, "Pastor, don't orders come down and not up?" He stated, "Yes, but you can carry out this task since I am instructing you." Immediately, I knew then that he had no vision. I stated to him, "Pastor, I mean you no disrespect, but did not God give you the desire to pastor this flock?"

He said yes! I further asked, "Why are we doing this without a vision statement from you?" He got upset with me because I was standing on the Word of God. I was reminded that this man had worked for Fortune 500 companies and knew the meaning of what vision and mission statements were. I did not want him to think that I intended to take over so I just put my head down and began to pray.

He then stated, "I see you are still on the vision kick, so you write it."

I wrote it, but it was never used. I did not fight with him, but I later realized that some people have been called to preach, but not pastor. The Bible clearly says that he will give you pastors after His own Heart…. that is, those with vision, and insight. Many people who say they are pastors are clearly not. They tend to be jealous of those who are secure in their calling. They may have the gifting to preach, but not to pastor. I have noticed from the Scriptures that David, the man after God's own heart, knew he had a calling on his life after Samuel anointed him king (I Samuel 16: 1-13). He was not concerned about kingship until he was of age and understood the vision. He continued tending to the sheep that his father had placed in his care. He was not concerned about what had just taken place with the ceremonial anointing by Samuel, the prophet. However, he continued to tend to the sheep as appointed (although there were two kings at this time on the throne). We all should be concerned about God's plans for our lives and not position, status or power. God is the one who will grant the promotion if we continue to be faithful in the "Now" and are not concerned about the "Later."

Many pastors have a tendency to say they have been called to pastor, but in essence, the whole issue is that of prestige and notoriety. Some will even say, "This is my church, my choir, my people…my this, and my that." So the question that lingers in mind…are we under a bunch of so-called preachers who have deemed themselves as pastors? A visionary pastor sees potential, growth and aspiration for future endeavors. He or she says, "This is not my Church, but God's." There is a fundamental difference that comes along with a pastor that has vision and one who has no vision; that is, either planning or preparing others for the next dimension in God's Body.

Vision lends itself to developing character and is not worried about how things will work out, but knows that God will work everything out as he or she writes what God is speaking to them. In Habakkuk Chapter II, he had deep concern about how the people of God were being treated. He was perplexed and given to a state of uncertainty. He, along with the Children of Israel, was in bondage for seventy years and questioned how the heathen Babylonian nation would ease their abuse. Habakkuk gently stated (author's interpretation) "I am not going to move or cause a riot, but I will stand still until I hear a word from God."

That's all we need in our troubled lives is one Word from God that will change our lives. Pastors who are prone to take a step without God's leading can open the door to chaos and discord. When uncertainty is in our midst, pastors or any person for that matter should not be moved, but do exactly what Habakkuk did and that is, "Stand there and write down the vision that God gives them." Writing things down causes a person's mind to be thoroughly and concretely steadfast in what God tells them. I know in times of hardship; many people have tendencies to ask or consult with others on various subject matter to get understanding regarding what should be done (this is wisdom according to Proverbs 11:14). Questions like, "Where do I go from here?" "How do you think I should handle this? Or, "When do you think it is time to move?" However, we must be reminded that everyone does not have a Word from God. Sometimes other pastors can be mal-informed or mal-assigned to give a clear or clarion word to other pastors and believers. This consultation can sometimes foster or cause a disastrous situation and leave you wondering, "Was I called to pastor or not?"

Chapter 3

Did I Get on the "I" Plan or God's Plan?

"You sure can speak well," said the lady, "I know you are going to pastor one day because you speak so eloquently and with passion." Someone else stated, "You sure are an anointed man of God. You made those people get up and clap and shout with jubilation." Then the church said, "Man, did not pastor preach today!" These are statements to build the ego. Some pastors are egocentric and not God- centric. Some preachers and pastors do not care about the shouting and hearing of accolades. Nevertheless, there are some preachers and pastors who want to make sure that the Word of God is rooted in the hearts and minds of men. Whereas, some look for all the shouting, jumping of pews and the hand claps. That is rubbish! God instructed me a long time ago, "As long as a life is changed and some godly wisdom is shared and a soul is touched, then it is up to God to yield the increase of your labor (I Cor. 3:6 AMP)."

I remember one time hearing a pastor say to me, "I preached so hard that the ladies started jumping pews." Later he said, "And then the church took up five thousand dollars and gave it to me! Notice his statement, "I" preached so hard. It was never in reference to the moving of the Holy Spirit and giving God thanks for all He had done. Some pastors or preachers judge others in this manner. Egocentric preaching has made its way into the church in many ways. It is one of the prime ways or methods people can lose their authority, respect and utterly lose the leading of the congregation. This is the type of preaching that gives credence to arrogance and haughtiness. The Scripture says in Isaiah 13:11 *"And I will punish the world for their evil, and the wicked for their iniquity; and I will cause the arrogance of the proud to cease, and will lay low the haughtiness of the terrible."* This Scripture lets us know the demise of proud people. We have to be careful about those who say, "I did this, I sure was good, I am better than them," because it only fosters a wicked attitude and does not give respect to our gracious Lord.

The "I" plan is not a trait that pastors or preachers should have or any one for that matter. It only makes people become worldly or carnal in their thoughts and brings about a false sense of reality of what life should be. I have seen pastors who have four members in their congregation and were so faithful to those four that God promoted them. Another view is that those who had several members were made low because they were not thankful and humble for those He entrusted to their care. Come on, pastors, stop acting high-minded and let God do the elevating (Psalms 75:1).

Chapter 4

Don't Punk Out!

This area speaks to the heart of pastors and leaders who have others under their care. Sometimes they start counting how many heads they have in the congregation and think that more financial blessings will be placed in the basket. David did this when he starting to do a census as to the number in his army. He had to repent and had to pay Araunah for using his threshing floor to get back in God's good graces. Read this portion of Scripture that describes this incident when you start taking for granted what God has given you and start getting the big head. Then you will not "Punk Out."

II Samuel 24: 10-17 (AMP)" But David's heart smote him after he had numbered the people. David said to the Lord, I have sinned greatly in what I have done. I beseech You, O Lord; take away the iniquity of Your servant, for I have done very foolishly. When David arose in the morning, the word of the Lord came to the prophet Gad, David's seer, saying, Go and say to David, Thus says the Lord, I hold over you three choices; select one of them, so I may bring it upon you. So Gad came to David and told him and said, Shall seven years of famine come to your land? Or will you flee three months before your pursuing enemies? Or do you prefer three days of pestilence in your land? Consider and see what answer I shall return to Him Who sent me. And David said to Gad, I am in great distress. Let us fall into the hands of the Lord, for His mercies are many and great; but let me not fall into the hands of man. So the Lord sent a pestilence upon Israel from the morning even to the time appointed; and there died of the people from Dan even to Beersheba 70,000 men. And when the angel stretched out his hand upon Jerusalem to destroy it, the Lord relented of the evil and reversed His judgment and said to the destroying angel, It is enough; now stay your hand. And the angel of the Lord was by the threshing floor of Araunah the Jebusite. When David saw the angel who was smiting the people, he spoke to the Lord and said, Behold, I have sinned and I have done wickedly; but these sheep, what have they done? Let Your hand, I pray You, be [only] against me and against my father's house."

There is a cost to be paid for Punking out. **Punking out** is simply failing to be a good steward of that with which God has entrusted you. You automatically start taking members and leaders for granted and think that they will always be with you. This is only setting you up for failure. I remember a situation in which a pastor had several members who were gifted in the church. He would not let them carry out the gifts that they had and they in turn had to get permission before going to help other ministries. I heard them say, "I cannot come to help feed the homeless at your church today because my pastor said I could not." These were faithful servants to the body of Christ. It seemed as if there was a spirit of jealous hovering over the pastor of that local body because he had such a strong hold on the members. I understand the respect factor that is involved, but this scenario made it seem as though they were back in slavery.

We have to remember God has under-shepherds over the flock that is being pastored and not lords. The gifts and talents were given to the body of Christ and not to one specific church. I understand that the pastors have to give an account of the souls that are under their care, but should not be lords over them, as stated in I Peter 5:3 (AMP): *"I warn and counsel the elders among you (the pastors and spiritual guides of the church) as a fellow elder and as an eyewitness [called to testify] of the sufferings of Christ, as well as a sharer in the glory (the honor and splendor) that is to be revealed (disclosed, unfolded):Tend (nurture, guard, guide, and fold) the flock of God that is [your responsibility], not by coercion or constraint, but willingly; not dishonorably motivated by the advantages and profits [belonging to the office], but eagerly and cheerfully; Not domineering [as arrogant, dictatorial, and overbearing persons] over those in your charge, but being examples (patterns and models of Christian living) to the flock (the congregation). And [then] when the Chief Shepherd is revealed, you will win the conqueror's crown of glory."*

I have seen this view of "Punking Out" in many churches because the pastor started the ministry and he or she never takes time to look at the gifts that God placed in the congregation. The pastor cannot do everything by himself. That is why God has placed others there to assist. Punking Out brings about a view which states: "Since I am in control, no one can tell me what to do because I am the pastor." Just think about your own personal encounter with your pastor or preacher. Some think that pastors are the only ones used by God and the ones that control the people of God. As the Amplified Bible so adequately utilizes this Scripture in I Corinthians 14:32-34: *"For the spirits of the prophets are under the speaker's control [and subject to being silenced as may be necessary], For He [Who is the source of their prophesying] is not a God of confusion and disorder but of peace and order. As [is the practice] in all the churches of the saints (God's people).*

I know this Scripture mentions the fiduciary responsibility of dealing with the Church concerning speaking in tongues, prophesying and other gifts; however, it does have some revelatory knowledge as well concerning a pastor having those subjected to their authority. Some pastors may take the mind-set that they have members and say to them, "You do as I say and not what God has called you to do." This is in direct disrespect to the calling and gifting that God has given to the body of Christ to help perfect the Church until He returns. This is seen in plenty of churches and it causes the members to be perplexed and dismayed about when and how to use their gifting. I know I have experienced this in some of the churches that I have attended and it caused great pain for the members. Sometimes pastors do not know what to do and there are members in the local body that have been endowed with gifts that can further assist the pastor. Moreover, the pastor's jealousy stigmatizes the gifts, talents and abilities of members placed in the body of Christ.

I must admit that I have experienced this on a number of occasions and it made me want to leave that local body (some of them I did). Others made me feel as though I wanted to have a "Come to Jesus Meeting" where I could just give them the worst beating of their lives. However, I sat back and watched God deal with them on His own accord.

No matter how they hurt me, I listened and sometimes I said words that angels are even afraid to utter (God is still working on me). The key to this situation is to ask God to order your steps in leaving so that your gifts can be of use or you can stay there and be miserable. It is your decision; please pray before you allow flesh to take control.

Chapter 5

All I Want Is to Help Lift Your Arms

"Then came Amalek [descendants of Esau] and fought with Israel at Rephidim. And Moses said to Joshua, Choose us out men and go out, fight with Amalek. Tomorrow I will stand on the top of the hill with the rod of God in my hand. So Joshua did as Moses said and fought with Amalek; and Moses, Aaron, and Hur went up to the hilltop. When Moses held up his hand, Israel prevailed; and when he lowered his hand, Amalek prevailed. But Moses' hands were heavy and grew weary. So [the other men] took a stone and put it under him and he sat on it. Then Aaron and Hur held up his hands, one on one side and one on the other side; so his hands were steady until the going down of the sun" (Exodus 17: 8-12 AMP).

As I walked to my pastor's office and saw his door opened, he beckoned me to come to speak with him. It was all about the new ministry over which he had assigned me to serve and administrate. He stated to me, "You're very good with the people, but do not get caught up with the drama in some of the ministries."

I politely asked him what he was referring to and he stated primarily the "Women's Ministry." I did not know what he was truly talking about so I asked him to expound further on the issue at hand. He did elaborate and then he stated that he was going to take this ministry from me and place his wife over this ministry. I stated, "I do not mean you any disrespect, pastor, but your wife never taught a class and never attends anything that the Women's Ministry has planned for the year." I then sensed that he had a hidden agenda to take a ministry that was not part of that local body and place it under a not-for-profit that was not related to our local church. The conflict was not with me but his wife, who did not get along with the other ladies who had thoroughly planned out the ministry for the entire year, and she was very jealous. I stated to him, "All I wanted to do was to hold your arm so that you would not have all the pressure on you."

He stated, "I am the pastor, and I know how to do my job." It was apparent that he now had a problem with me and the ladies because of the well laid plan that was devised by his wife who never attended anything in ministry. We had a sit-down meeting with other ladies who had been coming to the meetings and got ideas regarding what they wanted to see done for this ministry, but because the pastor's wife was not the head and money was involved, he allowed his arms to become weak. He never asked me to include his wife in the forefront. He was only interested in making money and making sure that his household, not the house of God, was taken care of. I did not argue with him, although I did not agree with his actions. They were crafted and designed to benefit part and not the whole of the ministry for the women.

He took this ministry from under my supervision and gave it to his wife. Thereby, strife and chaos was the end result. In turn, none of the women in the church were being helped or any women that were affiliated with our local church. All I wanted was to hold up his arm and serve as a type of help in this vital role. By my helping him, it would ensure he would not get tired with all that he had to accomplish.

God quickly allowed me to see that some pastors do not want their arms to be held up, due to pride and self-conceit. The women's ministry was no longer active because he let his arm down. This is what happens when a pastor who does not have true vision needs someone to hold his arm up while in battle. Chaos, confusion, back-biting and utter killing of people's spirits are the main result. I have come to realize that if he had only allowed me to keep doing what I was doing and holding his arm, then all of the aforementioned issues would have never happened. I was at the top of the hill watching to see if the enemy was going to come but he now became the "All Seeing Eye" and did not allow me to help him. His actions caused a rift in our relationship. Although I was not angry with him nor did I hold any grudges, he began to treat me as if I was not part of the church family. Although he never said anything else to me, his actions and mannerisms gave way to what truly was in his heart. I sat there Sunday and Wednesday continuously, until I could not hold his arm any longer. My hands began to get tired and my mind weary of his non-verbal communication until I had to leave that local body.

As the Scripture reference implies, Moses needed some help and could not continue to hold up that rod until the end of battle. He needed Joshua, Aaron and Hur to assist him. As you noticed in the verses, Moses never uttered a word of negativity against the help. He knew he needed help if he wanted the battle to be won for the Israelites.

However, this is a very important moment in the life of the nation of Israel. As they journeyed toward the Promised

Land, they were faced with their first encounter with some of their enemies. The Bible tells us that they came face to face with the armies of Amalek. These people were a nomadic tribe that was a constant thorn in the side of the people of Israel. In this first encounter, they prove their nature by conducting an unprovoked attack against the Israelites. This prompts the Lord to promise the total annihilation of the Amalekites. This promise was later fulfilled.

In this scene from the travels of Israel, we find the great leader Moses mentioned, along with Aaron, as well as the first mention of the future leader, Joshua. All of these men were great leaders in the history of Israel and all played a very important role in the early history of this great nation. However, there is another man mentioned in these verses that deserves our attention: his name is **Hur**. This is a man who steps out of nowhere, does a great work and then disappears into the same shadows from which he came. He did not want a church, prestige or any accolades. All he wanted was to see that God's people win this battle.

Pastors, we need you to have the attitude of Hur as unsung heroes who are often unnoticed, un-thanked and underappreciated. People who perform a function in the Body of Christ that is so vital, but never get the recognition they deserve. People who enable the rest of us to do what the Lord has called us to do, that is those who make up the front line, yet are not looking for the limelight. I am not saying all pastors want to be in the forefront. If Jesus is not the center of any action, then all our efforts are in vain.

In the Church, there are still found the Moses', the Aarons and the Joshua's. There are still those people who get the credit, those who get seen, those who do the headline grabbing work of the ministry, but behind every one of those people, there is an army of Hurs. There are a vast number of people who are praying, fasting, and carrying the load so that the first line people are able to do their work.

People who pray and seek the Lord's face and lift up the hands of those who are weary in the Lord's work are absolutely indispensable.

I remember one Sunday after service; people would come up and tell me they enjoyed the message. Those words did help me, and the people were blessed. People tried to give me the credit. However, I knew that everything good that I had ever done, or the Word of God being preached or taught, was from the Lord. I also knew that every time I stood to preach, there was some saint of God who spent time in prayer on my behalf. Nothing means as much to me as those most precious people of God who are lifting me up in prayer. I want you to know, I understand that I need those who stand in the gap for me and are not out in front! The world may never know your name, but if the battle is ever to be won it will be won by the saints of God who are winning the victory in the closet of prayer as they lift up their hands and hearts for me and for those of us who constantly teach and preach the Word of God.

There are many in our churches today that are just like Hur. They are invisible to the crowds. The preachers, the teachers and the singers all get their pats on the back and hear people say, "Well done!" However, there are people like Hur who remain invisible and are never heard.

Moreover, there are some disadvantages to being like Hur: *It is often a thankless task*. People like Hur work and labor, yet no one ever says, "Thank you!" It can be hard to keep serving the Lord when it seems that nobody appreciates what you are doing for God or the pastor. It is times like these that reveal our true motives and identity. The sermon may be great and the preacher may have done a good job delivering it, but behind him or her are the many saints who sacrificed their time to pray for the message and the messenger. The preacher gets the credit, and the real workers go unnoticed. Again, this may be hard for some to deal with, but may I remind you that while humans may not see all that you are doing down here for the glory of God, the Lord in Heaven is keeping a perfect record and He will one day reward you for your labor.

As I examined the Scripture a bit further, I noted that Aaron, Joshua and Hur were so quick to think about keeping the hand of Moses and the rod up that they had uniquely placed a rock to assist them. Sometimes, it is not only the hand-holding that is needed; it is the quick and savvy thinking of others that keeps pastors out of trouble and jail cells. The rock showed how God not only used their physical bodies, but their minds. Some pastors do not want us to help hold them up, even with our ideas, because it is not their idea. However, we still can pray for them.

You may not have a high profile position. You may think that cleaning the church, praying for the services, or teaching your small class is an unimportant function. It is not! May I remind you that others are watching. There are people who are not saved who are watching how you serve the Lord in your position. There are little ones who will see whether mom or dad is faithful in the little things. There are no unimportant duties in the church. The wise follower knows that his life is an investment. As we do the little things God gives us, we are telling all those around us that God's work is important in every detail.

In times of distress, some would wish they had listened to the wisdom of those who do not carry a baton to lead the people in a parade. Many of us have pure motives and only want to hold our pastor's hands so they will not stumble and suffer the rigor of ridicule and laughter. I write this portion not out of sympathy but out of the sheer goodness of my heart. I hope one day that some pastors who are standing on the top of the hill and looking back will remember this phrase… *"All they wanted was to help lift my hands!"*

Chapter 6

Saul: The Distressed and Possessive King

"And David went out wherever Saul sent him, and he prospered and behaved himself wisely; and Saul set him over the men of war. And it was satisfactory both to the people and to Saul's servants. As they were coming home, when David returned from killing the Philistine, the women came out of all the Israelite towns, singing and dancing, to meet King Saul with timbrels, songs of joy, and instruments of music. And the women responded as they laughed and frolicked, saying, Saul has slain his thousands, and David his ten thousands. And Saul was very angry, for the saying displeased him; and he said, They have ascribed to David ten thousands, but to me they have ascribed only thousands. What more can he have but the kingdom? And Saul [jealously] eyed David from that day forward. The next day an evil spirit from God came mightily upon Saul, and he raved [madly] in his house, while David played [the lyre] with his hand, as at other times; and there was a javelin in Saul's hand. And Saul cast the javelin, for he thought, I will pin David to the wall. And David evaded him twice. Saul was afraid of David, because the Lord was with him but had departed from Saul (1Samuel 18:1-12 (Amp)."

King Saul had the honor of being Israel's first king, since other nations had one. His life turned into a tragedy for one simple reason: Saul did not trust God. Saul looked like royalty: tall, handsome, and noble. He became king when he was thirty years old and reigned over Israel forty-two years. Early in his life he made a drastic mistake. He disobeyed God by failing to completely destroy the Amalekites and all their possessions, as God had commanded. The Lord withdrew His favor from Saul and had Samuel the prophet, anoint as king. Because the people made more of David's single victory than all of Saul's, the king went into a rage and became jealous and distrusted David. From that moment, he plotted to kill him. Instead of considering the nation of Israel, King Saul wasted most of his time plotting and chasing David. David, however, respected God's anointed king and despite several opportunities, refused to harm Saul. He knew he was anointed as king of Israel but he stayed loyal and true to Saul.

Finally, the Philistines gathered for a huge battle against the Israelites. By that time, Samuel died. King Saul was desperate, so he consulted a medium (or a witch) and told her to from the dead. Whatever appeared—perhaps a demon disguised as Samuel, predicted disaster for Saul. In the battle, King Saul and the army of Israel were overtaken. Saul committed . His sons were killed by the enemy.

Saul was impulsive and acted very unwisely. His jealousy of David drove him to madness and a thirst for revenge. More than once, King Saul disobeyed God's instructions, thinking he knew better. That it is how the modern day pastors can become when those who are under their leadership have been anointed to teach, preach, minister and carry out the work that God has designed for them. The instinctive impulse of jealousy causes many pastors to run off those who are only there to help carry out the mandate that God had for the entire ministry. When pastors are distressed and have allowed a demonic force to overtake their minds, then other issues abound such as rudeness, haughtiness, revenge, selfishness, utter panic and the major consequence--being dethroned from office.

I have seen this on many occasions where pastors do not want another minister, deacon or lay person to do anything because they are afraid that the other person's passion for the ministry will overshadow them. This is why you have to be rooted in Christ and what he has called you to do. The enemy likes discord and his main motive is to steal, kill and destroy (Matthew 10:10). *Pastors must realize that some people do not come to take from them, but to help them restore that which has been taken.* If a pastor knows who he or she is in Christ, then there is no need to 'throw a javelin' at others from the pulpit or even utter words that make others feel like their gifts are not appreciated. This is why there are so many local buildings or churches on every corner in our communities. This is not to water down the fact that God does sometimes call people out of a local assembly to make sure that the body of Christ's needs are fully met. Some ministries start out of hurt and some start out of splits. I have witnessed this and the pastor becomes so possessive that he or she deems themselves the "Pastor for Life." No information is passed on to the congregation, financial statements are hidden, the membership is left in the dark concerning the vision of the local body and, most of all, the money being taken up is pocketed. No ministries are ever carried out except Sunday School and worship service.

The insensitivity of these pastors leaves members with a lackluster view of how God wants His people to operate. They should not be afraid to come to the pastor with new ideas and special sessions that God has given them. I have heard pastors say, "Not in my church." It is all because they did not come up with the idea. Our God is an all-unifying God. He shares gifts, talents and abilities as He sees fit. I do not understand this point of view when the pastor knows that the person's real intent is only to try to assist him or her with "The Great Commission" (Matthew 28: 19-20).

I remember a scenario in which I served as youth minister of a local body and God gave me this great idea that would allow the children, youth and families to come to the football stadium just like that of a Billy Graham Crusade. My pastor at that time said, "Write me a plan of action and see how we can get the entire church body to help." As he blessed the plan of action and the church came on board, many people were helped, some accepted Christ, and local churches in the area of all denominations came out without hesitation to assist. It was because God blessed it first, and my pastor was not intimidated. He wanted to see people come together to fellowship and especially evangelize and disciple. However, I am seeing a new dynamic of pastors who only want programs and ideas to come from "them" … Thus, the "I" plan once again. This is a terrible misfortune that some pastors are so selfish that they think of themselves as a type of "god." I am not trying to mock or ridicule any pastor, but if this fits you, then repent and ask God to help you in this area of your life.

Chapter 7

Jealous Leaders Can Cause Division in the Kingdom

"And the women responded as they laughed and frolicked, saying, Saul has slain his thousands, and David his ten thousands. And Saul was very angry, for the saying displeased him; and he said, they have ascribed to David ten thousands, but to me they have ascribed only thousands. What more can he have but the kingdom? And Saul [jealously] eyed David from that day forward. The next day an evil spirit from God came mightily upon Saul, and he raved [madly] in his house, while David played [the lyre] with his hand, as at other times; and there was a javelin in Saul's hand. And Saul cast the javelin, for he thought, I will pin David to the wall. And David evaded him twice Saul was afraid of David, because the Lord was with him but had departed from Saul. So Saul removed David from him and made him his commander over a thousand; and he went out and came in before the people." 18:7-13 Amp.)

Jealousy is a rash human emotion created when a person feels insecure or anxious about his or her value to other people. When jealousy occurs, it puts a strain on relationships and causes problems. People could side with one person over another, which ultimately leads to bitter statements, gossip, sabotage and even bullying.

It should have been a day of great celebration. Israel had defeated the threat against their national security. Goliath was dead, and his army was defeated. Saul's army was victorious in battle and the women came to cheer the soldiers as they returned home, but their song did not please the king. 'Saul has killed his thousands,' they said, 'and David his ten thousands!' Instead of rejoicing with the crowd at David's success, Saul became jealous and insecure.

When Goliath defied the Israelites, Saul had his armor with him and he was quick to loan it to David, but was not willing to adorn it himself to protect his kingdom. When David came up with a plan and volunteered to help, Saul was eager to criticize his plan and belittle David for offering to help, but never did he say to the shepherd boy, "No, I'll do this, it is my place not yours." As far as I'm concerned, David had a vision for getting the job done more efficiently than Saul had ever thought or even fathomed. But as soon as the fighting was over, Saul wanted to ride at the front of the parade. He was trying to get the credit for something he really did not accomplish. However, the women were hospitable to Saul. They could have said, "Saul has really nice armor that he is willing to loan to men with courage, while David has courage that needs no armor." Instead of being angry that David was included in the song, he should have been grateful that the generosity had any reference to his name at all. But we all know human nature, and I do not think a single person here is surprised by Saul's reaction.

Before the women greeted the men from the battlefield, Saul appeared to be pleased with David and was elevating him through the ranks. In effect, he gave him a battlefield commission, making him a commander. The more seasoned soldiers and officers took no offense in the promotion. They did not become jealous of David's success; instead they were pleased with it. Moreover, David had killed their most fierce opponent, Goliath. I'm sure they were proud to serve under a man of such honor and dignity, even if it meant they had to follow a younger, less experienced man. Saul's men were able to do what he could, but they never voiced any negativity about it even if they thought it. But it was only their leader who had the wherewithal to say and do so. David's success meant they were successful too. Unfortunately, Saul could not comprehend that when a man under his command distinguished himself, it reflected well on his country, his fellow soldiers and on the king. Instead, Saul chose to become jealous and caused utter chaos in the kingdom.

The next day, Saul tried to kill David, even as David was ministering to him. Saul grabbed a spear and threw it at David, intending to pin him against the wall. David leaped out of the way and ran for his life. Why would Saul try to kill his son's best friend? Why would he try to kill his armor bearer-his bodyguard, and a commander in his military? He had morbid jealousy-the kind of jealousy that kills.

We must remember that pastors who are not secure in themselves can destroy a local church. Although there are much younger and invigorating preachers around, the "Sauls" of this world should be glad to share and not be selfish. I know many preachers that have store front churches and can preach me under the table, but it is not about that or me. It is about the Kingdom of God. When we get so consumed with the experience of other preachers or pastors, it only causes much more chaos for the "Church." So what if someone prays well or preaches well. God is not concerned about how well we pray or preach…but that we are praying and preaching.

This is one of the main problems in the modern day church. The "Saul mentality" in the church is trying to kill God's plan, but it will never happen. Before he allows the "Sauls" of this world to raise their heads, He allows the ultimate plan of defeat. Just because some gave another preacher or pastor accolades, why should I get upset? I should be happy that another brother or sister in Christ is doing what is required of them and God honors them with even small conjectures such as, "You are a wonderful preacher, thanks for a job well done!" Or, "you sure did explain that well, my fellow minister." Sometimes the inner thoughts that lurk through the crevices of the heart have a way of manifesting themselves in some tangible way that will create problems for the local Church. Sooner or later, the real you will come out. It may take a week, two months and even years, but God still knows how to deal with confusion.

I remember when I finished delivering a message one Sunday and one of the members came up to me as I was talking to the Senior Pastor and said to him, "I wish you preached like Michael." I immediately said, "Please do not say that. I thank you, but we have a great pastor here as well." The pastor turned his head and walked off and I never got a chance to deliver another sermon at the church again.

Insecurity is like a fire that burns down an entire house and there are no remnants remaining…no bed to lay one's head, no food to salvage and no clothes to wear. It has a way of weighing heavy on people's minds every time they see that person coming around. Insecurity will yield no "thanks or congratulations" as a way of inspiring that person to continue working and doing greater works in the Kingdom of God. But I am steadily reminded that God tells us in Psalms 75:5-6, (author's interpretation) "I will promote you and set down those who are not prepared to receive promotion."

Notice in the main Scriptural reference, the women's comments never gave David the "big head." I could see him riding in behind Saul with a faint smile and yet humble in his way. As many times as I have read this Scripture, I never saw where David responded. David wanted King Saul's vision to go forth in defeating Goliath but instead, Saul issued a boomerang with jealousy and javelin causing more damage to his kingdom.

I stopped saying the old cliché: "If you dig one ditch you better dig two." If I am doing right and honoring God, I will not fall, but the one who is digging the ditch will ultimately fall. I have learned in my years of preaching that the anointing of God will protect you, and promote you in due season but most of all, as Proverbs 18: 6 states, "A man's gift maketh room for him and bringeth him before great men."

Chapter 8

Excuse Me Pastor, the Gifts Are from God and Not from You!

"And His gifts were [varied; He Himself appointed and gave men to us,] some to be apostles (special messengers), some prophets (inspired preachers and expounders), some evangelists (preachers of the Gospel, travelling missionaries), some pastors (shepherds of His flock) and teachers. His intention was the perfecting and the full equipping of the saints (His consecrated people), [that they should do] the work of ministering toward building up Christ's body (the church),[That it might develop] until we all attain oneness in the faith and in the comprehension of the full and accurate knowledge of the Son of God; that [we might arrive] at really mature manhood – the completeness of personality which is nothing less than the standard height of Christ's own perfection – the measure of the stature of the fullness of the Christ, and the completeness found in Him. So then, we may no longer be children, tossed [like ships] to and fro between chance gusts of teaching, and wavering with every changing wind of doctrine, [the prey of] the cunning and cleverness of unscrupulous men, (gamblers engaged) in every shifting form of trickery in inventing errors to mislead (Ephesians 4:11-14)."

I have read this Scriptural reference many times and God has always given me a new revelation with its interpretation. His gifts and callings are not with repentance. I must say it is not the pastor that calls people to have these gifts. Although it seems to be relegated to the pastor's own perception in the reading and studying of this passage, it is blatantly clear. My beloved pastors, it is God that gives and takes away. Why do some pastors think that they have the reins? Why do they imagine that they can control people who are called to operate in these areas? It is God that mandates when these gifts become active and useful in the local Church.

The gifts are subject to God and not man alone for the perfecting of the members of the Church. This is a grave injustice to those who have been uniquely called to these positions when they are not allowed to utilize them. I know you might be saying, "Brother, the pastor is the under-shepherd."

Yes, I do know this, but God is the ultimate Shepherd. I have seen many pastors who are intimidated because someone in the church can teach or preach better than he or she. However, we must remember this is not a contest in Christ. All of these gifts are given to the body of Christ to make the Church more efficient when dealing with life issues. If the pastor would only move out of the way and let these gifts flow, then and only then will we have a more cohesive and unified local body.

I must admit that jealousy is killing the local membership due to the fact that some pastors will not relinquish the power and allow these people to operate in their calling. I know that some may be novices in their gifts and may need some training, but true training only comes by allowing each of them to utilize their gifts and, if mistakes are made, then the pastors can use their rod of love and kindness to help make these gift(s) better.

When I acknowledged my calling to the preaching ministry, my pastor called me into his office and stated, "I will not help you with your first sermon but afterwards I am there for you." At first, I thought this was very uncharacteristic of a pastor. I felt that he was being mean and cruel. I later realized that he was allowing God to flow through my life and, if I made any fleshly mistakes, he would be there to help and assist me. He was not threatened, nor was he intimidated by my gift. He was from the "Old School" that stated that I needed to have a "burning and learning" for the area in which I stated I was called. Although I did make some mistakes and we did not agree on everything, he took me under his wing and showed me the correct way to hone my gifts to be a blessing to the body of Christ.

Some people may call the above Scripture "The Five Fold" Ministry. It is never mentioned in Scripture that way. The five gifts are only a "snapshot" of what God can give to the body. However, there are many more gifts and talents that the Holy Spirit births when needed. Some people may have these gifts mentioned above in the local church but some pastors do not have a discerning spirit to know if they are there or not. This may be one reason some pastors feel threatened, because they do not understand who God has placed in that local body. I am not being judgmental by what I am about to say. You can tell if a pastor is anointed for the position of pastor or not by their negative or positive expressions, tone, mannerisms, lack of growth in the body, and lack of a written vision. Some pastors might think that because they have a large congregation it's a sign that they are anointed. That is not always the case. A large membership is not a sign that the pastor is working diligently to help that local body grow. It could be other reasons why people are there such as: family, love for other members, the church may have a good choir, other ministries are operating well, or there may be some other leader(s) in that church who are really teaching, preaching and evangelizing. They are the ones doing what God has called them to do and people are coming to hear them teach or preach. I have come to realize that, unlike in the past, you now have a more informed and intelligent membership. Nevertheless, some pastors will tell you: "I am the pastor and you are not" or "God called me and not you." This is a very bold statement for the pastor to make. Excuse me, pastor, we do not want your local church! We want excellence in the body of Christ.

Excellence is one of the priorities that God is seeking. He longs to see members assisting and helping those pastors who may not have the gifts mentioned above. As mentioned earlier, there are many more gifts that are not mentioned in the Bible. Some pastors may not understand that Ephesians 4:11-14 is a mere template which one uses as a starting point and later God adds more talents and gifts. Every person that is born into this world has at least one talent and some more. Moreover, a talent is not a gift until it is turned over to the anointing of God; and the Holy Spirit blesses that talent, because it is being used specifically for God and His body. That is when the talent becomes a gift. He actually places "His Super" on our "Natural" which enables us to carry out His work. Pastors and members need to stop saying some things are not of God. God is ushering new thoughts, ideas, patterns and ways to perfect the body. I know that one of the gifts that

I have is that of administration. I know how to organize and make sure things flow under the dictates of the Holy Spirit. If I did not use my gift correctly, then I could cause chaos in everything I began to do in the church and could also cause dissension.

That does not mean I should go into a local church and take over. In essence, I should ask the pastor what is the vision for that local body and is there any way that my skills, talents and gifts can help this ministry flourish. We do not need pastors who do not have vision that does not come from God. We need pastors that encourage vision and foresight to spring forth from the Holy Spirit. That is why you may see many people "Church-hopping" because the gifting of vision is not at a local body. Am I saying that each pastor should be endowed with every gift? *No!* But he or she should ask God to give them vision to help carry the vision out for that local ministry.

In regards to "Church-hopping," it has become more apparent today due to lack of vision, gifts, talents and, mainly, mere jealousy. There is enough room in the Church for each of us to have something to do even if it is being a doorkeeper in the house of God. I do admit, I have gotten upset because I thought some of the pastors that I have been under should have grown and developed the people with whom God entrusted them, but I now understand…everyone does not have the same gift. These pastors were not trained themselves, nor did they take the time to embark upon getting some training or allowing someone with certain skills to come help educate and train the church where they served. I also cannot get upset because the pastor does not understand where and how to place people in a local body. Some pastors do not have discernment to know what gifts are operating in that local congregation. It is sometimes because pastors are not well-versed in areas of gifts and talents. They may not be able to discern what gift is needed and who has the right spirit with their gifting. If a mature believer knows what he or she has been called or assigned to do, then there should not be any room for trouble. They should simply operate in that which God has called them to do and should perform it well.

In other words, the pastor should not be the choir director. He or she should not be the usher. He or she should not be the drummer or organist when all these abilities are within arm's reach and anointed by God. Sometimes I believe pastors have what I call "take-over spirits" and want to control everything from the pulpit to the pew. If you see a pastor preaching, playing the piano, leading every song, teaching every lesson, directing the choir, ushering and then counting the offering…this is a sheer sign he or she has a "take-over spirit or a spirit of control." We all need to learn how to stay in the lane where God has called us. If I know I cannot play the piano skillfully, then I should not be making some ungodly noise and frustrating the ministry. We all have seen this and sometimes do not have the decency to realize we are not called to serve in that capacity. We should seek out what God's true plan is for our lives.

Chapter 9

Excuse Me Pastor, I Don't Want Your Pulpit...I Have My Own!

"And Ezra the scribe stood upon a pulpit of wood, which they had made for the purpose...Nehemiah 8:4"

I remember a pastor telling me to get out of his pulpit because it was his and his alone. I was a bit frustrated because I viewed myself as a called man of God and indwelled with God's Holy Spirit. What made him think that he was better than I and the piece of wood standing in the center? It caused me to look at that statement a little deeper and I came to the realization that he could not take it to heaven or to hell for that matter. It was a piece of wood.

I do understand that we should cherish and value the sanctity of what it was created for, but that statement caused me to think introspectively about what a pulpit really is. Is it really the wood piece or something that I was missing—something I was not told before I started preaching the Gospel of Christ? I started asking many of my friends in the ministry about it and they blatantly said that maybe the preacher or pastor was jealous of me. I was twenty-one years of age and ministering. I had preached several sermons and revivals and many people came to a saving knowledge of Jesus Christ. It still bothered me to the point in which I needed clarity. I prayed and prayed about it. I came to church Sunday after Sunday and no women were allowed to speak from that "wooden piece" and that further caused me to wonder if was there some special power in that piece of wood. I began to think that it was a child-like object like that of "Wonder-Woman" and her lasso.

Before I tell you what God gave me about what a pulpit really is, I think that it is necessary that we do a quick study on the origin of pulpits and how they came into being.

In some churches, the pulpit is considered the most important piece of furniture in the sanctuary. It is located centrally in relation to the congregation and raised. It is where the stands and may be decorated with a ''- a piece of cloth that covers the top of the pulpit and hangs down the front. Flowers may also stand in front of the pulpit.

In the eighteenth century, triple-decker pulpits were often introduced in English-speaking countries. The three levels of lecterns were intended to show the relative importance of the readings delivered there. The bottom tier was for community announcements, the middle was for the gospel, and the top tier was reserved for the delivery of the sermon.

In many , there are two speakers that stand at the front of the church. Often, the one in the center (as viewed by the congregation) is called the pulpit. Since the Gospel lesson is often read from the pulpit, the pulpit side of the church is sometimes called the *Gospel side*.

The other speaker's stand, usually on either side (viewed by the congregation), is known as the . The word *lectern* comes from the Latin word "lectus," past participle of legere, meaning "to read," because the lectern primarily functions as a reading stand. It is typically used by lay people to read the Scripture lessons (except for the Gospel lesson), to lead the congregation in prayer, and to make announcements. Because the epistle lesson is usually read from the lectern, the lectern side of the church is sometimes called the *Epistle Side*. In other churches, the lectern, from which the is read, is located to the congregation's left and the pulpit, from which the sermon is delivered, is located on the right (the Gospel being read from either the center of the sanctuary or in front of the altar).

Gaylon Embrey stated in his article *The Pulpit*, *"The primary problem with the pulpit, however, is not its abuse or misuse as a church auditorium fixture, but rather has to do with the "Pulpit" as an idea, in what it represents to the modern mind. Another of the several dictionary definition of a pulpit is "Preachers as a class," or "the preaching profession."* You can easily see how this word has come to be a figurative expression denoting those whose "profession" is preaching. As pointed out earlier, being made for each other, preaching and the pulpit have been united in marriage, joined together as one idea. Therefore the pulpit speaks of the preacher. Specifically, it refers to the Preacher-Pastor-Priest system of the denominational world.

In the contemporary Church world "pulpit" is a word symbol used with, or in contrast to, its partner word "pew." It is well understood in the nomenclature of Babylon that "the pew" refers to laymen, and "the pulpit" refers to clergymen. Moreover, anyone familiar with the situation knows that the distinction between clergy and laity is a very important, official distinction within these sophisticated church systems. The "step" up from the pew to the pulpit is much more than a matter of working up a Bible lesson and presenting it on Sunday. It is more or less a legal step that can be taken only by the guiding hand of denominational authority. Only a person who follows the necessary procedures for "entering the Ministry" can take this important step upward. Once taken, however, he becomes not just a person but a Parson, a "person" of the pulpit, a man of the Cloth, a bona fide PREACHER! Organize him just right and he may be tax deductible!"

Moreover, the pulpit is an elevated place or enclosed stage, in a church, in which the clergyman stands while preaching and giving a message. The Scripture mentioned above never mentioned any special powers that it had but that of Ezra (the Scribe) and other men who stood upon it too for its purpose. That purpose was to read what the scribes had written during that time. Some older pastors think of the pulpit as holy ground like that of Moses when he encountered God and God told him to take of his shoes (Exodus 3: 5). In that case, how come we as ministers do not take off our shoes to give reverence to that Scriptural passage? I say that not to belittle the thinking of some pastors but to reflect my belief that it has gone too far with this concept of "My pulpit."

As I stated earlier, God has given me a deeper revelation on what the pulpit really is and how we as believers should view it. God allowed me to understand that a *"pulpit" is a place where preachers, deacons, elders, laymen, and Christians all are working together to "Pull those from the Pit of hell."* Each of us as Christians has our own pulpit that God has given us to preach from. Your pulpit may be at work, dealing with a nagging boss or co-worker, or maybe a spouse that does not know who Jesus is. We have so desensitized the church to holiness because we are worldly in our thinking and how we look at things. I know some people may read this portion say, "There he goes again, this man has lost his mind." No!!! I just think it is time for us to be real about the things of God and let us focus on the weightier matters of life.

The Word of God backs this up by saying many "Woes" to this stinking thinking of the Scribes and Pharisees in Matthew 23:13:30: *"But woe to you, scribes and Pharisees, pretenders (hypocrites)! For you shut the kingdom of heaven in men's faces; for you neither enter yourselves, nor do you allow those who are about to go in to do so. Woe to you, scribes and Pharisees, pretenders (hypocrites)! For you swallow up widows' houses and for a pretense to cover it up make long prayers; therefore you will receive the greater condemnation and the heavier sentence. Woe to you, scribes and Pharisees, pretenders (hypocrites)! For you travel over sea and land to make a single proselyte, and when he becomes one [a proselyte], you make him doubly as much a child of hell as you are. Woe to you, blind guides, who say, if anyone swears by the sanctuary of the temple, it is nothing; but if anyone swears by the gold of the sanctuary, he is a debtor [bound by his oath]. You blind fools! For which is greater: the gold, or the sanctuary of the temple that has made the gold sacred? You say too, whoever swears by the altar is not duty bound; but whoever swears by the offering on the altar, his oath is binding. You blind men! Which is greater: the gift, or the altar which makes the gift sacred? So whoever swears by the altar swears by it and by everything on it. And he who swears by the sanctuary of the temple swears by it and by Him Who dwells in it. And whoever swears by heaven swears by the throne of God and by*

Him Who sits upon it. Woe to you, scribes and Pharisees, pretenders (hypocrites)! For you give a tenth of your mint and dill and cummin, and have neglected and omitted the weightier (more important) matters of the Law—right and justice and mercy and fidelity. These you ought [particularly] to have done, without neglecting the others. You blind guides, filtering out a gnat and gulping down a camel! Woe to you, scribes and Pharisees, pretenders (hypocrites)! For you clean the outside of the cup and of the plate, but within they are full of extortion (prey, spoil, plunder) and grasping self-indulgence. You blind Pharisee! First clean the inside of the cup and of the plate, so that the outside may be clean also. Woe to you, scribes and Pharisees, pretenders (hypocrites)! For you are like tombs that have been whitewashed, which look beautiful on the outside but inside are full of dead men's bones and everything impure. Just so, you also outwardly seem to people to be just and upright but inside you are full of pretense and lawlessness and iniquity. Woe to you, scribes and Pharisees, pretenders (hypocrites)! For you build tombs for the prophets and decorate the monuments of the righteous, Saying, if we had lived in the days of our forefathers, we would not have aided them in shedding the blood of the prophets."

I do believe that we as pastors, preachers, teachers, and laymen need some "woes" in our lives to get us back in the reality of godly thinking and not the thinking of our own. I cannot apologize for the Word of God but we do need some correcting every now and then. There is too much judgmental thinking in the house of God. Moreover, God sometimes may speak to us as my deceased father would tell me when I acted up and he gave me the rod of correction: "It may not feel good to you, but it is good for you."

Chapter 10

Excuse Me Pastor, I Understand That I Am Not the Senior Pastor

In a church meeting the pastor of this local church stated to me… "I know how to handle this finance issue and besides, I am the "Senior Pastor" and you are the associate pastor. It really disturbed me that he had this mentality of "I know it all." He actually had an authentic and fake set of financial records being recorded at the same time. In essence, when the fake information came before the church body, the finances were incorrect and the pastor was ashamed to admit that his information was incorrect.

This situation is very confusing, but all too familiar in our churches. Some pastors seem to think that they are the accountant, the auditor and the clerk, but do not realize the vulnerable mindset that it places them in, not only of spiritual torment, but also in physical jail cells with those that we label as criminals.

I was searching and googling for material on this section and I came across an article by , associate pastor, Lancaster Baptist Church in which he discusses the following: "Not all of us as preachers are called to be a senior pastor. If God has called you to be what is I call the 'second man or woman,' then in reality, that's first place for us. We may wonder if this is what God has for us for the rest of our lives, but when we come to the conclusion that we are exactly where God wants us, then we will not even entertain other opportunities. It is that sense of *contentment* in our heart(s), knowing that we are in God's will, and then we are free to love and embrace our position as the assistant.

Being the "second man or woman" is not an easy position to fill. We all have an ego; we must die daily. We must remember that God's ministry is not about us. We must strive to put aside our own agenda and selfishness. When our pastor gives us some extra work, and we want to say, "My day is full," remember that it is not our time to be senior pastor, but the one that is behind the scenes, helping and uplifting the senior pastor.

As a servant leader, we must strive to avoid a position-oriented approach to life. Leaders have influence by encouraging. We do not have to have a special title in order to have influence. Additionally, when we are not out to gain a specific Position, our motives become pure. Our decisions will become based upon God's will, not our own. When we are in the right place and right position, God will bless, and we will be fruitful.

If we are in a second position, we must truly understand and embrace that role. In God's eyes, the second position is not any less important than the position of a senior pastor. If the second position is God's calling upon our lives, then we must receive it wholeheartedly. Moreover, assisting the senior pastors to fulfill the vision that God has given to them does not in any way diminish our value for the cause of Christ.

Sometimes this role is somewhat of an internship, preparing us to serve as senior pastors later. Other times an associate or assistant pastor's role is simply administrative in nature to free up the senior pastor to focus more on teaching, preaching, and discipleship.

It should also be mentioned that the specific words "associate pastor" or "assistant pastor" are not found in the Bible. Given this thought, associate or assistant pastors work as leaders in the church, serving alongside the senior pastor, with Jesus as the Head of the church. That thought should be advantageous for every person in leadership, to recognize that the church belongs to Christ, to recognize that He is the Head of the church), and to recognize that a leader is really a servant who has not come to be served, but to serve others.

This view further brings about another aspect of church leadership which is described in (which you can read at your leisure). Furthermore, there are other verses that refer to the duties of elders and what is expected of us. For example, the elders bring order into the church: *"For this reason I left you [behind] in Crete, that you might set right what was defective and finish what was left undone, and that you might appoint elders and set them over the churches (assemblies) in every city as I directed you"* (AMP).

Also, the elders, especially those that teach, are to be supported by the ministry, if possible: "Let the elders that rule well be counted worthy of double honor, especially they who labor in the word and doctrine" ().

In addition, elders are to be examples to believers, feeding them with the good doctrine of the Word of God as they serve. And they are rewarded for their service. *"I warn and counsel the elders among you (the pastors and spiritual guides of the church) as a fellow elder and as an eyewitness [called to testify] of the sufferings of Christ, as well as a sharer in the glory (the honor and splendor)* that is to be revealed (disclosed, unfolded): Tend (nurture, guard, guide, and fold) the flock of God that is [your responsibility], not by coercion or constraint, but willingly; not dishonorably motivated by the advantages and profits [belonging to the office], but eagerly and cheerfully; Not domineering [as arrogant, dictatorial, and overbearing persons] over those in your charge, but being examples (patterns and models of Christian living) to the flock (the congregation). And [then] when the Chief Shepherd is revealed, you will win the conqueror's crown of glory (I Peter 5: 1-4) AMP."

The elders also have a ministry of prayer, and prayer is, of course, important in any ministry. An example of the type of prayer pastors should offer up on behalf of their congregations is Jesus' high priestly prayer in , where He prays for all His disciples to be protected from the evil one, sanctified by the Word, and made perfect in Him. Although not specifically mentioned in Scripture, associate/assistant pastors are to be as other elders: strong in the Word of God, strong servants, and men of prayer. Below are some ideas to help fulfill the role of an assistant pastor:

1. <u>Recognize the Pastor's Vision</u>

You must be able to trust your pastor's vision and acknowledge that it has come from the Lord. Know the pastor's vision by listening to the pastor in meetings and in his or her preaching, by spending time with them, by asking appropriate questions, and by praying for them.

Understand the pastor's vision—understand its importance, its ramifications, and your role in fulfilling the vision. Our goal is seeing the vision become a reality. Ask God for wisdom in how to answer questions about the pastor's vision. People will ask staff members questions that they would not ask the pastor. Remember what you say will be repeated. Be extremely supportive of the direction that the pastor is going because the church will be watching your response.

2. **Receive the Pastor's Vision**

Each staff member must fully embrace the vision of the pastor. Remember that God has given this vision to the pastor, God has led you to be part of the staff to accomplish God's will through the pastor, and God has gifted you to be an active player on the team. Additionally, embracing this vision will include not only your actions, but also your attitude. Choose to be excited about your pastor's vision, even if it is not what you think it should be.

3. **Reciprocate the Pastor's Vision**

The pastor should not be the only one voicing the vision. Each staff member plays an important role in communicating the pastor's vision to those in their realm of influence. In venues we might be participating in such as: an adult Bible class, choir practice, to school parents, etc., we should be voicing what he is voicing, and be as excited or more excited than he is.

4. Reflect the Pastor's Vision

Reflect the vision through excitement, through participation, and through your spirit. Your spirit is contagious. Be excited about what God is doing!

5. Reevaluate the Pastor's Vision

The pastor lives with the vision and the burden 24/7. We should try to walk in their shoes, but I really cannot fathom it all. Sometimes we only know a small portion of the entire picture when the pastor does not communicate the full vision. This is where the problem lies. It should be fully communicated by the senior pastor and all associate pastors should evaluate their hearts regarding the vision, embrace the vision continually, and share the excitement for the vision.

6. Resolve to Help with the Pastor's Vision

Stay personally committed to the vision. Make sacrifices each year to give more and do more. When we are committed, we will find ways to get things done. Stay personally connected in fulfilling the vision. Ask them for help in preparing the visionary statement. Sometimes pastors cannot communicate what they truly want to do and this is where the chaos or the breakdown in communication occurs. It may be a hard task to pull the words out of them and sometimes they may not like what you have to say, but it's better to say it now rather than later. This will streamline any unforeseen problems and, should there be problems, it is ok to go back to recant some of our statements verbally and on paper.

7. Reassure the Pastor of His Vision

The pastor will need our love, loyalty, longevity, and labor. It's our choice to give the pastor support. Ask God to help us to be the man and woman of God that our pastor can count on, and seek to serve God by serving as our pastor's right hand man, the "second man."

With these seven points, I am sure that we can assure ourselves and the pastor we are simply servants and not trying to take over. It is simply our honesty of heart if we do not agree with his or her vision. If so, pull them aside and address the issues that we are having with the vision. There is no need to make it a catastrophic conversation. Sometimes they may not understand what we are trying to explain to them, but learn to use soft words and a gentle spirit to achieve the clarity that is needed in the vision. This will foster a more harmonious relationship with them whether they are male or female pastors.

Chapter 11

Excuse Me Pastor, Are You Intimidated or Jealous?

I was invited to speak for one of the special days in a church. As I walked up to the pastor of this local church and tried to introduce myself, he immediately said to me, "Remember, I am the pastor and you are just a preacher!" I responded humbly by saying, "I appreciate you and all the good work that you are doing for the Kingdom of God." I knew this was a spirit of intimidation. Normally, when you have visiting ministers come to speak to a local body, they offer you the center church in the pulpit area. He did not! He said, "You sit right here and I will take the middle chair." This was so hilarious to me because I was confident in who I was in Christ. As I finished preaching the message, many people came to shake my hand to tell my how they enjoyed the message. The pastor of the local church got up and walked out and went to his study. He did not say "thank you" or "I appreciate the message" nor were there any compliments or saying of "amens" during the message. It did not bother me because I was focused and I knew my purpose. I always knew that if your purpose is known, it clearly gives credence to any negative vibe that permeates from any person, place or thing.

I had ministered at this local church many times and the congregation would always ask that I come back to speak again. This time was very different. I remembered the last time I visited, several people gave their lives to Christ and many others rededicated their lives to the Lord. It was not because I was "Holy Ghost Junior." It was because the anointing of God landed on fertile ground. God caused growth and change was fostered in the minds and hearts of men.

The way the pastor of that local church acted was a sheer sign of intimidation or jealousy. Pastors have to realize that God can use anyone to change the tone or atmosphere anywhere the Word of God is being spoken when everyone is in one accord. As stated in Acts 2: 1-21, *"And when the day of Pentecost was fully come, they were all with one accord in one place. And suddenly there came a sound from heaven as of a rushing mighty wind, and it filled all the house where they were sitting. And there appeared unto them cloven tongues like as of fire, and it sat upon each of them. And they were all filled with the Holy Ghost, and began to speak with other tongues, as the Spirit gave them utterance. And there were dwelling at Jerusalem Jews, devout men, out of every nation under heaven. Now when this was noised abroad, the multitudes came together, and were confounded, because that every man heard them speak in his own language. And they were all amazed and marveled, saying one to another, Behold, are not all these which speak Galileans? And how hear we every man in our own tongue, wherein we were born? Parthians, and Medes, and Elamites, and the dwellers in Mesopotamia, and in Judaea, and Cappadocia, in Pontus, and Asia, Phrygia, and Pamphylia, in Egypt, and in the parts of Libya about Cyrene, and strangers of Rome, Jews and proselytes, Cretes and Arabians, we do hear them speak in our tongues the wonderful works of God. And they were all amazed, and were in doubt, saying one to another, what meaneth this? Others mocking said, These men are full of new wine. But Peter, standing up with the eleven, lifted up his voice, and said unto them, Ye men of Judaea, and all ye that dwell at Jerusalem, be this known unto you, and hearken to my words: For these are not drunken, as ye suppose, seeing it is but the third hour of the day. But this is that which was spoken by the prophet Joel; And it shall come to pass in the last days, saith God; I will pour out of my Spirit upon all flesh: and your sons and your daughters shall prophesy, and your young men shall see visions, and your old men shall dream dreams: And on my servants and on my handmaidens I will pour out in those days of my Spirit; and they shall prophesy: And I will shew wonders in heaven above, and signs in the earth beneath; blood, and fire, and vapour of smoke: The sun shall be turned into darkness, and the moon into blood, before the great and notable day of the Lord come: And it shall come to pass, that whosoever shall call on the name of the Lord shall be saved."*

Noticed I bolded two words prior and reiterate them again "One Accord" which means it is not "I", "Me", "You", but the two words which mean "all inclusive." I am not writing to talk about speaking in tongues nor to decide who has received the "Holy Ghost" but to simply express how God will allow His Spirit to move when we are together. So many things can be accomplished if we are together.

I do not know what happened to the pastor of that local church, but I knew God moved that day and His Spirit brought newness to the people of God. There is so much that can be done when we stop thinking that it is 'all about us' and not about God doing the work through us. Pastors and lay people alike must understand that it is the duty of the Church to carry out this work.

I later came back home and thought about how petty the pastor acted and it caused me to look at life very differently. Although I was preaching that day, I wondered who else saw the attitude of that pastor. We should all remember that our actions, mannerisms, and even our speech have a way of reflecting how we really feel. The way we act as Christians can cause a great divide in church, especially our pastor. I also thought about the members who saw the pastor leave the church without speaking to me. He put on his coat and hat and got in his car and never uttered a word and the members were amazed at his actions. The above scenario is how intimidation and jealousy work.

Intimidation and jealousy are cousins to each other. They feed off of the "misery loves company" concept. Especially when a pastor uses intimidation, it causes members not to become active. They become stagnated, with no vision, and, most of all, division. A spirit of dwarfism evolves (i.e. no growth of members being added to the church)

I believe the best way to handle intimidation is to use some points that I wrote in my other book "Walking in Heavenly Authority" and they are: "Know your Position in God, Know your Present Victory in God and Know your Power in God (John 4:4, Philippians 1:28, II Corinthians 10:4)."

The enemy is the author of confusion and division. If he can keep the leaders in the church divided, they will not minister effectively. However, since pastors usually have the oversight of local churches, there is a need for understanding and unity between the laity as well.

At the heart of any strife between pastors is often the need for control, usually brought about by personal insecurity. When pastors have other gifted people in their local church, they must not allow insecurity and intimidation to grip their spirit. If it does, then they will perceive everything any member does as a challenge to their authority. Strife and division will eventually be the result.

Conversely, the laity should be careful how to handle situations reserved for the pastor of the church. The pastor has the responsibility for the souls of the sheep. Pastors also bear the responsibility for the spiritual oversight of the entire membership that comes under their tutelage. Often, the enemy causes a war between the pastors and apostles and prophets. The pastors feel intimidated by the manner in which God uses the apostles and prophets, and the apostles and prophets feel that the pastor is against them and does not understand their ministry or accept them as ministers.

Obviously, the need for good, clear channels of communications is very evident and vital. Without good communication, there will be confusion and no one will benefit but the kingdom of Satan. Pastors have to resist opposing or fighting those with other gifts in the local membership in an attempt to feel that they are in control. Control should not be the issue ministry should be the heartbeat of every church. Furthermore, a key point is that other ministers have to learn to be subjected to leadership if they expect to have fruitful ministries within a local church.

We must remember that there is a need for all gifts and ministries in the Body of Christ. Pastors cannot devalue the diverse gifts that God has given to other ministers, prophets, preachers, teachers and evangelists because they are, in some ways, under the covering of their leadership at that local body. Pastors need to understand that these ministries are foundational and are an asset to any ministry and there is no need for intimidation or jealousy.

Furthermore, other leaders cannot feel that they are "above" the pastors because of the authority and anointing upon their lives. Ministries are given to work together in peace. It is with this understanding that apostles, prophets, and pastors have to work together in the local church or assemblies. This will mean taking time to understand one another.

Two main areas need to be explored and understood. First, the personalities of leaders besides the pastor must be thoroughly understood. Personalities can certainly affect the way ministers are able to work together in unity. However, it is simply necessary to recognize that God has given each of us different personalities and all people involved need to understand. Many may not function, think, or feel the way we do. After all, if we were all alike it would be boring. And, if we all thought exactly the same, then most of us would be redundant.

Secondly, we need to work together to understand the unique perspective of the leaders and positions in the church. The pastors always sees things through the eyes of the shepherd who wants to lead and guide their sheep gently so as not to lose one. The story of Jacob returning to his homeland after fourteen years and meeting up with his brother Esau has a tremendous bearing. As the two brothers are reconciled Esau suggests they move quickly together into the homeland. Jacob states that his brother should go on ahead of him because he must care for the sheep and go as slow as necessary so that even one new born lamb would not be lost (Genesis 33:13). Pastors should be cautious, caring and not intimidated. However, they often move much more 'slowly' than other team members would like because they do not understand each leader's personality and this causes much chaos. Although it is not wrong, pastors must recognize that each leader has a natural proclivity to move faster with the vision than they; and, thus, this is where the problem sometimes lies.

The ministers, however, will see things from God's vantage point. They also hear from God and see what "can be" and "should be" with less concern for "what is" than the pastor. The pastor can be somewhat narrow in focus, concentrating on what he or she has seen or written. What has been revealed to them from God may take time through fasting, prayer and meditation before they act. Whereas, other leaders are focused on obtaining what they heard the pastor say and they grasped it quickly. This can sometimes mean that pastors are seen as very narrow-minded and somewhat unconcerned for the sheep. Where the pastor would *lead* the sheep, ministers and other leaders often seem to *push* them because their focus is on what God wants to achieve and how things should look and not on the status quo or how the change that is needed may affect God's people. The pastor can then become even more intimidated and jealous.

I remember I was member of a local body and the pastor had given all the members directives to carry out a specific task. We had our plan and due diligence was in order as we gave it to him. But he said to us, "I did not tell you all to do this."

It was like a spirit of amnesia had set in. If I did not have the minutes from the prior meeting he would have grown even more hostile and intimidating. That is why I learn to write everything down when I am in meetings of any kind so that people will not go into a sort of when the vision or plan is given to the leader. He then said, "I now remember I told all ministers to do this," and from that point on he was very intimidated toward me because I was prepared and diligent about the skills God had given me. Moreover, I have learned that though other ministers may see what God wants to accomplish, some do not have all or any administrative skills to help the ministry grow.

This further envelops intimidation in the pastor because, once again, they do not understand some gifts God has given other ministers and lay people in the local church. The pastor should see the need to teach and lay foundations so that all sheep are allowed to feel secure. The minister or lay person will work diligently toward the vision if the pastor's vision is lacking. Moreover, the local body will suffer from dwarfism in their spiritual growth. The pastor should be apt to teach, counsel, train, equip, and lay foundations so that what God wants can actually be obtained in a healthy manner.

The pastor sees the sheep and then the vision of the Lord. Other ministers see the vision of the Lord and the current situation of the Church. They also see the church as it is and as it must become, and they build a bridge between the two. Because of these vastly different perspectives, misunderstanding is birthed and therefore confusion and chaos comes between all facets of the ministry team members. Therefore, time, effort, and a great deal of love, understanding, and patience is required to make this team function effectively and pastors have to be on guard for intimidation brewing in their lives that will further split the local body.

Chapter 12

Excuse Me Pastor, but You Are Lazy!

"And again Jesus spoke to them in parables (comparisons, stories used to illustrate and explain), saying, The kingdom of heaven is like a king who gave a wedding banquet for his son And sent his servants to summon those who had been invited to the wedding banquet, but they refused to come. Again he sent other servants, saying, Tell those who are invited, Behold, I have prepared my banquet; my bullocks and my fat calves are killed, and everything is prepared; come to the wedding feast. But they were not concerned and paid no attention [they ignored and made light of the summons, treating it with contempt] and they went away—one to his farm, another to his business, While the others seized his servants, treated them shamefully, and put them to death.[Hearing this] the king was infuriated; and he sent his soldiers and put those murderers to death and burned their city. Then he said to his servants, the wedding [feast] is prepared, but those invited were not worthy. So go to the thoroughfares where they leave the city [where the main roads and those from the country end] and invite to the wedding feast as many as you find. And those servants went out on the crossroads and got together as many as they found, both bad and good, so [the room in which] the wedding feast [was held] was filled with guests. But when the king came in to view the guests, he looked intently at a man there who had on no wedding garment. And he said, Friend, how did you come in here without putting on the [appropriate] wedding garment? And he was speechless (muzzled, gagged).Then the king said to the attendants, Tie him hand and foot, and throw him into the darkness outside; there will be weeping and grinding of teeth.

For many are called (invited and summoned), but few are chosen (Matthew 22: 1-14). "

People who know me understand that I sometimes operate in the prophetic gifting. I can tell when someone is lazy, especially in ministry. This should be very easy for us to see, but apparently, it is not. I do have a tendency to say what is on my heart when God leads me. However, I do not like the ways of lazy pastors. When I speak of laziness, I speak in the vein of those who are lazy in their duties to their local church in which they serve as under-shepherds. I am not shocked when I hear and speak to parishioners about their pastors. Now, I have done this enough to know that positive reactions usually go unnoticed. That is fine. Only the negatives draw responses as a rule. In other words, it seems as if the bad pastors do draw more controversy and negative responses than the good pastors. You may ask why I make such a statement. Each pastor has a flesh and when flesh is drawn to negative behavior it brings a negative light to the Church in general.

Several pastors to whom I've spoken about ministry state that they are not really lazy. They are simply a bit stressed or pressured and their quality of work suffers. I empathize with them. I have been preaching twenty plus years and stood in for pastors who are sick or even tired. I have been a youth minister for eight years, and served as a Director of Christian Education ten years, working with a vast number of people in the various churches as well as their pastors. I know about pastors being under stress, dealing with pressure, and being too sick to perform their duties. However, that is not laziness but a sign that delegation is needed. So, at the risk of offending a group of sincerely struggling pastors, I want to look at this chapter in a way that brings to the forefront and asks a question of every pastor that reads this book: Are you really lazy or do you just not want to pastor?

Some pastors cannot bring themselves to do the unpleasant tasks, but keep putting off the hard things. I once read that one of the greatest traits of successful people in the business world is that they make a list of their tasks for the day, and then tackle the hardest, most unpleasant ones first. That takes dedication, commitment, focus, which many pastors lack. Some even call their assistant pastor at the last minute and say, "Can you preach today, I may be running late."

Some pastors may use this as a scapegoat technique so they will not come off as lying or being ill prepared to minister that day, but in actuality, they are simply lying and are lazy.

I remember a pastor telling me at the last minute that I was up to minister. There was no schedule or no sickness in view. I knew he'd stayed up too late and watched the basketball game and just simply lied. I did minister because I was taught by one of older pastors that gave birth to me in the ministry to always be prepared. Again, this pastor just outright lied. I could see straight through it. If he did not feel like ministering, he should have looked at his schedule, realized that the game was coming up and called me a week before instead of two hours before church started. This was simply wrong! I did not say anything to him, but I do believe that he would have gotten up and fumbled the message like those on that basketball court he was "so-called watching." Moreover, I do respect leadership, but leadership needs to respect follow-ship as well and not use them as a wet mop. If he was tired, he should have said to me, "Minister, I am tired and I stayed up a little too late."

I would have appreciated that much more than just receiving a call two hours before church started. What a tragedy! I did not say anything to him in a negative way, but my non-verbal communication on the phone gave me away: "Excuse me pastor, you are being lazy."

Just as I am to be prepared, he should have been prepared as well. However, that type of pastor really does exist today!

Moreover, some pastors will not do any ministry that is easy or does not have an immediate payoff. If there is a need in the community, pastors such as this will often call some of the deacons and people in the neighborhood to help. Too often we, as associate pastors or preachers, have caused our pastors to be ineffective by not standing up and saying, "Pastor, I cannot do that today," letting them know that we have some responsibilities at our own homes or other duties that are needed at the local church.

I am sincerely writing from my heart. I have been used, abused and utterly attacked by pastors because they are in authority. Some have told me, "You will never give another message or teach at this church because you do not do as I say."

Anyone who knows me understands that ministering is on the crest of my heart; and there is nothing that I would not do to further the Kingdom of God, but not at the expense of enabling an impatient and lazy pastor. I do believe God called me to help assist pastors when needed, but not at the drop of a hat. It is not my job to get out of line and begin pastoring when there is already a pastor in place. God called them to pastor that local body; he did not call me. However, I would be willing to give all that I have to help bring a synergistic approach to helping my pastor. However, I will not contribute to making him or her lazy.

I am inclined to believe that one of the acid tests to see if a pastor is lazy or not is this very point: If pastors are always in the "begging mode" for other ministers to carry out services when they were called to pastor that church---they may be lazy. This might seem crazy in thought; but I must call it out, there are simply lazy pastors around us. Some pastors are late for weddings, funerals, Sunday school and other duties. It is not because they had an emergency. They were there to get the pay check, not for ministry. This may be hard corn to swallow. This type of pastor that does not put in the time should not be in line for a paycheck. This is definitely not their calling. I have seen some pastors dreading to come to their church where they were 'called' to pastor. Some pastors see most of their calling as a job and not a ministry.

At this point, the layman will ask, "Well, why would a man go into the ministry if he doesn't like the work expected of a pastor?" That is a good question. I have wondered that myself. But my observation is that the slothful shepherd gets no joy out of hospital visitation, crisis ministry, office administration, staff meetings, or sermon preparation. If they do not do them at all, it is apparent they are simply lazy or were not called to pastor, period. I have seen some pastors rush into hospital rooms, barely make eye contact with family members, utter a few clichés as in sermons, offer a prayer, and be on his or her way, relieved to have done it. Some of you who are not pastors see the same thing and are amazed to call them minister or pastor at all.

The fact is that many parts of the pastor's calling are difficult to most who say they are called, and they have to train and discipline themselves to do the task at hand. In the course of advising or counseling people, I have heard, seen and uncovered people who are on the verge of divorce, working through difficult jobs, advising members who have browbeating pastors, and it broke my heart. Where are the real and dedicated pastors who understand flawed sheep? Advising can still be draining—physically and emotionally—but it is what shepherds and ministers do. This may be hard a statement for me to make: "If you cannot overextend yourself or stretch yourself to do any of the above, then it is time to question your calling to the preaching and pastoral ministry. I know the above Scripture mentions the parable of a king who instructed his servants to call them that were bidden to the wedding and they would not come and he kept calling them and he ended the parable in this manner… "For many are called (invited and summoned), but few *are* chosen. (Matthew 22: 1-14)." Does this relate to you my fellow brothers and sisters in the ministry?

Chapter 13

Excuse Me Pastor, You Are Immature!

Let no one despise or think less of you because of your youth, but be an example (pattern) for the believers in speech, in conduct, in love, in faith, and in purity (I Timothy 4:12(Amp)."

When a pastor finds every excuse not to carry out his or her duty this can also be viewed as immature. Even the sermon topics that are used may be selected to try to get the attention of the people, but eventually the pastor will have to continue using those topics to keep the flock around. I went to this church and heard a sermon topic which was "The bloody woman and her cycle." I understood where the pastor got this topic, but many people started to walk out of the church service because the topic came off as very chauvinistic and immature. The pastor was homiletically unsound and unlearned. This caused great harm to many of the women in that local congregation. I can still hear the women talking about it today. Some said, "How dare he do that" and others whispered with grim looks on their faces and said, "Pastor should been on his knees praying as we are."

I know that the above Scripture relates to Timothy, a young pastor in the ministry; however, Paul encourages him as he starts his pastoral journey. The Scripture can also be viewed from the standpoint of pastors who are young or immature in their pastoral role. It does not matter how long a pastor has been pastoring, they can still be immature.

Some pastors are glad to find any excuse to get out of doing what God called them to do: "Oh, I'm so sorry. I will not be able to do that funeral. I have something else on my calendar." Some funerals a pastor can get out of officiating since the deceased was not a member of his congregation, or the beloved former pastor is able to drive back to town for the services. But in most cases, the pastor should do the funeral of all church members--even if the former pastor assists, or another pastor participates. A man or woman of God will want to be there to help the people.

This is not to say the minister should skip his child's ball games for every church committee meeting. But he will make sure to cover the essential aspects of his ministry and put things in perspective. If he has additional ministers on his staff, he should not try to do everything himself, but involve them.

Sometimes I have heard pastors say, "You do not want to study for your sermons. You would rather find a good sermon in print or on-line and preach it." Preaching someone else's sermon is never, ever, ever, a good idea. However, the Lord may speak to you through someone else's sermon and that could even furnish a great idea or even the bulk of your own message. But you must get the sermon from the Lord through your own prayer and study, and not from a book or website. A friend of mine asked me how I got my sermons. I immediately said, "I ask God to show me through His Word and I meditate on what I have gone through during the week."

He paused and looked at me with caution and said, "All that speaking that you do comes from God?" And I said, "Yes, and If you allow God to speak to your heart you don't have to pick up someone's sermons or use their phrases. God will give you a new a way to deal with His people and preach His Word." He nodded his head in agreement.

When God called me to preach, I did not try to be anyone else or to mimic my current pastor. I have come to learn that all you have to do is be you. God does not completely change your personality; He uses it for His Glory. You do not have to be like a noted pastor; just be who God called you to be! It takes drive and determination for pastors to be uniquely themselves. It's the same for anyone theoretically speaking. However, let me start with pastors, since judgment begins with the house of God and that judgment begins with us leaders. We crave validation or justification so much we will put on any persona we think will work or say things we think will help us appear and feel successful, popular, dynamic, attractive, and acceptable. We enter into "inappropriate relationships" with our congregations: women, men, children and others, to say the least, because we imagine we are ultimately beholden to them, dependent upon them. But the gospel of God's grace in Jesus Christ frees us from hypocrisy; it frees us to boldly own our inadequacies, our flaws, our failures, and especially our sins.

The immature pastor imagines himself really getting down to the level of the people he is trying to reach. He thinks he is really connecting with them. He is being authentic, transparent, and relevant. But that sort of self-consciousness is none of those things. What did C.S. Lewis say about humility? "Humility isn't thinking less of you; it is thinking of yourself *less*." And so in a curious ironic fashion, when we are trying so hard to "keep it real" or should I say most like the majority of the younger people (keep it 100) , we usually end up mired in pride, tempted to project an image or put on a persona that really that does not do us justice. Moreover, we fear and shudder at the thought that the real us would not be viewed as the way Christ looks but how we look to people.

What we need is real humility. Real humility consists of the boldness to be you. Also, to have the courage to say things in love that others might not say. Immaturity has no place in pastoral leading. It is one of the worst and most misleading attributes to have. It is a type of mask that is worn to a masquerade ball. It hides the genuineness of what a pastor should be. Am I saying a pastor should not have fun? Absolutely not! There is a time and place for all things.

I think of all the masking some pastors "put on"—the different faces in attempts to conceal their sin, weaknesses, insecurities, inabilities, and their utter ineptitude in an attempt hide from the people. I realize that while the masks of timidity and a mild psychiatric disorder characterized by anxiety, depression, or hypochondria might make them *look* humble, they are really self-centered and self-protective. And in that sense, many Christians are just as self-conscious as the pastor projecting himself as a king, and thinking in a prosperous way of fakeness instead of putting on humility — which is putting on Christ — however, frees us from both self-pity and projection. Breathing a sigh of gospel relief, I can be myself, whatever that means for whoever is watching. If God is for us, who can be against us, anyway? They can get glad in the same pants they got mad in. Pastors must strive to be all things to all people (I Cor. 9:22) without compromise. In the meantime, we should not forget that we are all human beings as well.

But we must understand it is God who approves us, qualifies us, commissions us, and loves us. We have been crucified with Christ, and it is no longer we who live but Christ who lives in us, and the life we live in the flesh, we live by faith in the Son of God who loves us and gave himself for us (, para.). As we mature in the faith, then, He increases and we decrease. And we can put the stupidity and immaturity away. They truly are not helping. We as ministers or pastors must remember that the gospel is fuel for the courageous un-self-conscious minded pastors and not for the immature.

And this is what people really need from us! The freedom to drop the pretense, to be radically un-self-conscious — not un-self-reflective, by any means, but un-self-concerned — and so liberated by God's approval of us in Christ Jesus that we are okay with owning our own immaturity

I was reading an article as I was prepping for this book and I believe it was an internet article (author unknown); it reads *"A former pastor pleads guilty to kidnapping and raping several women in a local county. The total verdict was three counts of kidnapping and three counts of criminal sexual assault, according to the judge presiding over the trial. As part of the deal, the pastor will spend 20 years behind bars, and must register as a sex offender.*

The pastor is accused of pulling a gun on the accuser, taking her to a trailer behind his church, and raping her. The guilty plea comes on the second day of the trial. According to the assistant solicitor, the three victims wanted the pastor to spend more time behind bars, but they "wanted closure" and are happy "they can all begin to heal." Wednesday's hearing in St. George started with testimony from a Verizon wireless specialist who examined the pastor's phone records. The pastor's attorney, Andy Savage, says the incident which his client is accused of was all part of a sexual fantasy and says the pastor and the accuser had prior contact before the alleged rape.

The specialist testified on Wednesday that there were some back and forth calls and texts between a phone number that was in the name of the pastor's wife and a prepaid number around the date of one of the alleged rapes in 2011. On Tuesday, the victim stated the pastor put a pillow case over her head, bound her hands, and then took the pillowcase off before raping her. The alleged victim denies the two had ever spoken before.

The pastor was a minister at a church in Ladson, S.C. when authorities arrested him in July, 2011. Authorities say the former pastor offered women rides, pulled a gun on them, and then put pillowcases over their heads. The pastor then drove the victims to vacant trailers, where the alleged sexual assaults occurred, according to investigators."

As I read this over and over, I have come to realize that the frailties of pastors and lay people everywhere sometimes speaks louder than the words spoken or messages we give. It is mostly humanity's proclivity which causes them to cover-up rather than simply stating, "Excuse Me, I Am Guilty." This would save families time, court costs and taxpayer money if we are honest and plead to the cause. David in Scripture was that way when Nathan had to reveal to him that he was the one who had Bathsheba's husband killed (II Samuel 11-12). Sometimes we have call things out or make pastors and leaders aware that they are not above the law.

Sin and guilt, confession and pardon are not exactly part of the apex of society's vocabulary. In fact, the word sin can be perceived as rather intimidating, even oppressive by our contemporaries or even our pastors. If people only knew that the biblical understanding of the human condition can be so liberating--indeed, it can help us come to terms with guilt much more effectively than the fixes society offers. In popular culture, guilt is typically treated from two different angles, the justice perspective and the medical perspective. All of us live in the tension of these very different perspectives. Most of us do not want to grasp the meaning of either idea. We'd rather run from the truth than say once again, "Excuse Me, I am Guilty."

Alcoholism is an oft-quoted illustration in this debate: To some degree we are inclined to deal with a person's drinking habit from the medical perspective. We grant that alcoholism may be--at least to a degree--a genetic weakness and should therefore be treated as a disease. However, we also realize-- genetic weakness or not—the alcoholic (or those consumed by alcohol) is accountable. Also, sexual misconduct can stand as a crime or it constitutes a real answer to what we call "abuse."

When it comes to dealing with guilt, the justice perspective stresses human responsibility. Here guilt can form a habitual pattern since it begins early in human existence. Guilt is normally used by pastors, parents and all people alike as a way of punishing and controlling a defense mechanism to bypass the system and get a pastor or anyone off the hook. The Justice model promotes and perpetuates "self-punishment." But sometimes the question that we as Christian and non-believers have asked is whether justice is really blind? Self-punishment is a natural response to the fear of greater punishment--if I punish myself, perhaps the authorities will forgo punishment. It is a well-known fact that punishment of self is self-destructive. It is over utilized. I am not trying to stray from a biblical stance that we should not punish those who sin. I have gotten many internal and external beatings that cause remorse for my behavior. The mind and the flesh work in tandem to tell us that we are right or just, but the conscience later speaks (if not seared) and says "I am guilty."

The medical perspective, on the other hand, encourages a flat-out denial. A person may say: "I am not to blame. It's genetic, or it's a social system issue." The phrase "I'm ok-you're OK" (transactional analysis approach) expresses this position well. However, suppressed feelings of guilt will likely find other avenues of expression, via anger and depression which further shows that we normal-thinking people have fleshly woes that are broken and damaged goods.

I can speak to both portions of the medical and justice perspectives since I was in the industry for over seven plus years. I have seen guilty people in a non-guilty setting and vice versa. The feelings of guilt (or denial thereof) are self-perpetuated. These patterns of self-perpetuation become a substitute for true change and personal spiritual growth. The Christian or Pastoral Care approach shows us a qualitatively more efficient way to deal with guilt. First, Christians acknowledge the reality of sin and guilt. The Christian message is clear: Sin is a human condition and guilt has a transcendent dimension--it is guilt before God! And only God can break and destroy the bondage of sin and guilt.

But the message does not stop there. The good news is that God's love is unconditional and God is working in and through Christ to break that bondage and restore humanity. Forgiveness is just as real as is sin and guilt. Forgiveness is received through *metanoia* (the NT Greek word for "repentance") which is literally translated "change of mind." A change of mind is the initial step in the change of direction.

On one hand, resistance to change in the religious realm makes sense. Remaining true to at least the essentials of one's religious beliefs stands as a mark of faithfulness (although agreeing on what is an "essential" almost inevitably results in disagreement). On another level, however, one could argue that change is at the heart of the biblical message.

The Bible does not typically use the word "change." It centers instead on the rich theological vocabulary behind the prefix "re" language such as rebirth, renewal, restoration, redemption, reconciliation, repentance. These words certainly signal change, though, and dramatic change at that.

Such language helps to address the ever-relevant question regarding change: Why? The words above share the assumption that: 1) God's original creation has been damaged by sin; 2) God is at work to overcome this damage; 3) God has invited us to participate in His work. These realities call for change on three levels.

On an individual or personal level, this change means that God has made it possible to heal our broken relationship with him. Part of this healing involves an ongoing process of rediscovering what it means to fulfill our high calling to "image" him within His creation.

On a corporate level, God's language means that we have the capacity to heal broken human relationships and build healthier ones. It means that we can live in authentic community that bears witness to God's ideal for community.

On a cosmic level, the biblical vocabulary for change envisions the extension of God's work to the entire creation. The individual and corporate life of followers of Jesus impacts even this arena as God "makes all things new" (Revelation 21:5).

Each of these areas, of course, requires further elaboration. For the moment, it is enough to acknowledge how far God's creation – including humanity – has fallen from its original glory and how long is the journey back. We human beings, who often resist change – and are the only part of the creation with much capacity to do so – introduced the fall. We also remain the only part of the creation honored by God to join in His counteractive response to the fall.

In the end, and even now, God is the mover of this grand story. If we are to answer His gracious call to join Him, we cannot follow the general pattern of human history. Arguably, we cannot even follow the general pattern of church history. In the journey from the present to God's promised future, change is a given, but what does it look like, and how do we get there? What are the primary obstacles in our path? Or are we just masking the process as pastors and Christians to be viewed in a theoretical sense. Immaturity or not, that is the question?

Chapter 14

Excuse Me Pastor, Are You on Death Row?

"Woe to the shepherds (the civil leaders) who destroy and scatter the sheep of my pasturing! Says the Lord. Therefore thus says the Lord, the God of Israel, concerning the shepherds who care for and feed My people: You have scattered My flock and driven them away and have not visited and attended to them; behold, I will visit and attend to you for the evil of your doings, says the Lord. And I will gather the remnant of My flock out of all the countries to which I have driven them and will bring them again to their folds and pastures; and they will be fruitful and multiply. And I will set up shepherds over them who will feed them. And they will fear no more nor be dismayed, neither will any be missing or lost, says the Lord" (Jeremiah 23:1-4)

In 1943, Wesley Amundson wrote a life altering article in the Ministry of International Journal for Pastors, <u>The Shepherd's Responsibility to Flock</u> *"As we near the end of time and approach the second coming of the Lord Jesus Christ, the dangers which face the church will increase. It is not the dangers from with-out, such as wars, persecutions, disrupting of territorial boundaries, lack of finance that will constitute our greatest peril. The condition within the church is that which we need to guard against most of all. God has a "little flock" scattered over the earth, made up of people from every land and almost every lan-guage. This flock constitutes His remnant church in the earth, and as such it is to be pure and holy, without spot or wrinkle. In it is to be found peace, love, joy, light, and power such as no other body of people enjoy."*

Just as God gave Adam charge over the earth, to keep the garden and to dress it, to multiply and fill the earth with fruit, so He has given His pastors charge over His flock, to keep it always, to love it, to protect it, to build it up so that the world may be filled with precious fruit when the husbandman shall come for the harvest. We fear the danger of "having a form of godliness, but denying the power thereof." While it is true that this danger may come from the carelessness of the people them-selves, yet I wonder if the ministers of the Lord, the pastors of the sheep, may not also be re-sponsible for some of the worldliness and luke--warmness which exists among *us* as a people.

It was the task of Jeremiah to call attention to the condition of the church in his day. With weeping and groaning he went about among the churches and called for a reformation. His words were not addressed to the people alone. They were directed to the leaders and to the pastors, as well as to the people. Read his words

"The priest said not, where is the Lord? And they that handle the law knew me not: the pastors also transgressed against me, and the prophets prophesied by Baal, and walked after things that do not profit" (Jeremiah: 8a).

"Woe unto the pastors that destroy and scatter the sheep of my pasture! Saith the Lord. Therefore thus saith the Lord God of Israel against the pastors that feed my people: Ye have scattered my flock, and driven them away, and have not visited them: behold, I will visit upon you the evil of your doings, saith the Lord" (Jer.23:1, 2).

This is strong language to use against those that proclaim the Word of God: "Feed my Sheep," as the Lord states through the prophet. Do we accept the counsel given to Israel by the Lord as applicable to Israel today? Are we much different from them or better than they were back then? Is not the root of apostasy strong among us today, also? Is there not too much backsliding? Are there not too many leaving the church by the back door while new ones are coming in through the front door? Wherein lies the answer to these questions? Are we not prone to take for granted that a certain percentage of persons who come into the church will fall out and leave the truth? And yet we continually talk about bringing back those who have apostatized. Why do they go out the back door? Will resolutions stop the leak? I am afraid not. What then shall we do?

It is my firm belief that the place to start is not so much with the people as with the pastors, the ministers to whom has been given the charge, "Feed the flock of God." The minis-ters are not necessarily to preach to the people constantly, for we have been told that too much preaching is one of the causes for the coldness and apathy which is seen in some of our churches. They must be *led* into green pas-tures, not driven. The prophet Ezekiel joins Jeremiah in calling upon the pastors to have a care for the flock. He records the follow-ing words which were given him from the Lord God:

"Son of man, prophesy against the shepherds of Israel, prophesy, and say unto them, Thus saith the Lord God unto the shepherds: Woe be to the shep-herds of Israel that do feed themselves! Should not the shepherds feed the flocks? Ye eat the fat, and ye clothe you

with the wool, ye kill them that are fed: but ye feed not the flock. The diseased have ye not strengthened. neither have ye healed that which was sick, neither have ye bound up that which was broken, neither have ye brought again that which was driven away, neither have ye sought that which was lost; but with force and with cruelty have ye ruled them. And they were scattered, because there is no shepherd: and they became meat to all the beasts of the field, when they were scattered. My sheep wandered through all the mountains, and upon every high hill: yea, my flock was scattered upon all the face of the earth, and none did search or seek after them" (Ezekiel 34:2-6).

What follows is a terrible indictment against the shepherds that "feed themselves" and "feed not the flock." While we may seek to apply these verses to the apostate priests of ancient Israel, or to the apostate ministers of Christen-dom today, at the same time we must face the question of their application to "Israel." The messenger of the Lord has placed some of the responsibility upon us as ministers. You and I must be willing to share the responsibility, even though that responsibility may not be pleasant.

"'Be ye clean that bear the vessels of the Lord.' The church will rarely take a higher stand than is taken by her ministers. We need a converted min-istry and a converted people. Shepherds who watch for souls as they that must give account will lead the flock on in paths of peace and holiness. Their suc-cess in this work will be in proportion to their own growth in grace and knowledge of the truth. When the teachers are sanctified, soul, body, and spirit, they can impress upon the people the importance of such sanctification."

"The watchmen are responsible for the condition of the people. Yes, We need a converted ministry and a converted people." This is a paramount need in perilous times. We who are to teach others what is meant by true conversion surely must taste the sweetness and the joy of this conversion ourselves. Specific sins are men-tioned here that are in keeping with the words of the prophets of old: "While you open the door to *pride, envy, doubt, and other sins,* there will be *strife, hatred, and every evil work."* What a terrible condemnation is to be found in the statement that, while Jesus seeks entrance into our hearts, yet we "are afraid to bid Him enter."

Is it not time that we, as pastors of the flock of God, should turn to Him with all our hearts, with weeping and with strong crying? Is it not time that we permitted the lowly Jesus to fill our hearts and do for us that which we can-not now do for ourselves? Surely the time de-mands a clean, pure, and holy ministry. We need intellectual men, yes, but we need spiritual men and godly women. When the two are combined, then God will be glorified through His ministers and He will clothe them with righteousness. The lame will not be turned out of the way and the wounded will not be left to die. Instead of a stream of people going out the back door of the church, we will see that volume lessened to a great degree. The people want to be led by spiritual leaders, and they will follow this type of leadership. The condition of the Church depends largely upon how the condition of the ministry is grounded.

Let us remove the blame for the worldly con-dition of our churches from others and take the guilt upon ourselves. Then let us seek the rem-edy, the only sure remedy—full and complete conversion of our own hearts. Note one more quotation that has to do with the type of min-isters which God does not need in His work. It is a daring statement, but a vital one, and the pattern for us to follow: "The self-sufficient, the envious and jealous, and the critical and fault-finding pastors can well be spared from His sacred work. They should not be tolerated in the ministry, even though they may, apparently, have accomplished some good. God is forced to move by men or means. He calls for workers who are true and faithful, pure and holy; for those who have felt their need of the atoning blood of Christ and the sanctifying grace of His Spirit."

Jesus took upon Himself man's nature, that He might leave a pattern for humanity, complete, per-fect. He proposes to make us like Himself, true in every purpose, feeling, and thought—true in heart, soul, and life. This is Christianity. Our fallen na-ture must be purified, ennobled, consecrated by obedience to the truth. Christian faith will never har-monize with worldly principles; Christian integrity is opposed to all deception and pretense. The man who cherishes the most of Christ's love in the soul, who reflects the Savior's image most perfectly, is in the sight of God the truest, most noble, most honorable man upon the earth.

May the Lord make us true pastors of His, so that we may lead the flock day by day in such a way that when He asks of us the ques-tion, "Where is the flock that was given thee, His beautiful and precious flock? "We may say with Jesus, "I kept them in thy name: those that Thou gave me I have kept, and none of them is lost." Then on that day soon to come, when

He shall give rewards unto His servants, we shall lay all our sheaves and accolades at His feet and give unto Him the praise for that which He has so wondrously worked out through us in the saving of the lost."

Moreover, in a present society that is focused upon and driven by emotionalism, many will interpret this passage within that societal context. Many will view the condemning and scattering of the sheep by these pastors as a method of hurting the feelings of the sheep. Some people will view the driving away of the sheep by these pastors as their manner of rudeness toward the sheep.

However, such a perspective of would not be accurate within the context of Jeremiah 23 itself. Even so, reveals our Lord's promise and prophecy unto Israel to provide them with godly shepherds and to lift and exalt the Messiah who will rule for their sake over the earth as *"THE LORD OUR RIGHTEOUSNESS."* Then in the chapter returns to the subject of condemnation against the ungodly pastors (for Israel – ungodly prophets and priests). Herein we find our Lord's definition concerning their ungodly practice of scattering, driving away, and not visiting the sheep. Furthermore, herein we find our Lord's fierce wrath against them for this ungodly shepherding.

The Price to Pay for Scattering His Sheep

First, the ungodly pastors are condemned for scattering the sheep of the Lord's pasture from the standpoint of disobedience to the Lord and His Word, and thus scattering the sheep from obedience to disobedience as some are today.

In , the Lord condemns them, saying, *"For both prophet and priest are profane; yea, in my house have I found their wickedness, saith the LORD."* Then in , the Lord continued his condemnation, saying, *"And I have seen folly in the prophets of Samaria; they prophesied in Baal, and caused my people Israel to err."* These ungodly pastors were not feeding the sheep with the truth of God's Holy Word. Rather, they were manipulating the sheep through their false teaching, to err from the truth. Indeed, our Lord's estimation of such scattering, that it is spiritual folly, ungodly wickedness, and profane leadership.

Second, the ungodly pastors are condemned for driving away the sheep of the Lord's pasture. Yet in what way were they driving away the sheep? They were doing so by strengthening the sheep in the ways of disobedience and rebellion against the Lord. In the Lord condemned them, saying, *"I have seen also in the prophets of Jerusalem a horrible thing: they commit adultery, and walk in lies: they strengthen also the hands of evildoers, that none doth return from his wickedness: they are all of them unto me as Sodom, and the inhabitants thereof as Gomorrah."* These ungodly pastors did not minister in order to call the disobedient to repent of their wickedness and to return unto the Lord.

Rather, they strengthened the hand of the disobedient evildoers within their wicked character and conduct. Indeed, they not only taught the sheep to sinfully disobey; they also taught the sheep to stubbornly remain in rebellion without repentance. This was the manner in which these ungodly pastors were driving away the sheep. The pastors were driving them away from repentance of sinful character and conduct unto settled and stubborn rebellion against the Lord.

Indeed, reveals the false message that these ungodly pastors were delivering unto those who walked in disobedience and rebellion. *"Thus saith the LORD of hosts, Hearken not unto the words of the prophets that prophesy unto you: they make you vain: they speak a vision of their own heart, and not out of the mouth of the LORD. They say vain thoughts unto them that despise me, The LORD hath said, Ye shall have peace; and they say unto every one that walketh after the imagination of his own heart, No evil shall come upon you" (vs. 17)*. These ungodly pastors were teaching those who despised the Lord through sinful disobedience and stubborn rebellion that they would experience *peace*. They were teaching those to walk after the ways of their own heart in rejection and rebellion of the Lord and His ways that the evil of the Lord's chastening and judgment would not fall upon them. Yet the Lord's true message to the sinfully disobedient and stubbornly rebellious was just the opposite, as revealed in – *"Behold, a whirlwind of the LORD is gone forth in fury, even a grievous whirlwind: it shall fall grievously upon the head of the wicked. The anger of the LORD shall not return, until he has executed, and till he has performed the thoughts of his heart: in the latter days ye shall consider it perfectly."* Even so, our Lord's estimation of such driving away is that it is spiritual profaneness and falsehood which only makes the sheep spiritually vain.

Third, the ungodly pastors are condemned for not visiting the sheep of the Lord's pasture. Yet in what way were they not visiting the sheep? They were not doing so by not calling the sheep unto repentance for their sinful disobedience and stubborn rebellion. In he confronted them with that which they should have been doing, but were not doing, saying, *"But if they had stood in my counsel, and had caused my people to hear my words, then they should have turned them from their evil way, and from the evil of their doings."* They should have visited the sheep with the call of repentance to turn them from their evil character and conduct. Instead, as was revealed in , they were visiting the disobedient, rebellious sheep with a false promise of peace and with a false denial of judgment.

Thus in , the Lord condemned these ungodly shepherds, saying, *"I have heard what the prophets said, that prophesy lies in my name, saying, I have dreamed, I have dreamed. How long shall this be in the heart of the prophets that prophesy lies? Yea, they are prophets of the deceit of their own heart; which think to cause my people to forget my name by their dreams which they tell every man to his neighbor, as their fathers have forgotten my name for Baal."* Yet again in the Lord condemned them, saying, *"Therefore, behold, I am against the prophets, saith the LORD that steal my words everyone from his neighbor. Behold, I am against the prophets, saith the LORD, that use their tongues, and say, He saith. Behold, I am against them that prophesy false dreams, saith the LORD, and do tell them, and cause my people to err by their lies, and by their lightness; yet I sent them not, nor commanded them: therefore they shall not profit this people at all, saith the LORD."* Indeed, these ungodly pastors caused the sheep to continue in spiritual error with their lies and with their lightness. They delivered a message of lightness, rather than a message of hardness. They delivered a false message to promise peace within wickedness, rather than a true message to call unto repentance of wickedness. Thus our Lord's estimation of this lack of biblical visiting is that it is spiritual lying and deceit that only steal the true Word of the Lord from the sheep and cause the sheep to forget the name of Lord.

I earnestly pray that I will never become like these pastors and any other pastor as well. I am greatly burdened that this nation is filled with many pastors who employ this type of leadership. I feel sometimes like Jeremiah: *"Mine heart within me is broken because of the prophets; all my bones shake; I am like a drunken man, and like a man whom wine hath overcome, because of the LORD, and because of the words of his holiness () ."*

We as ministers and pastors really need to watch what we are saying to the sheep of God. We will have to give an account to those that are under our leadership. No matter how much clout, money, or prestige the people in our congregation may have, we need to stop prophesying a lie. I call this type of prophet a "Parking Lot" prophet. They only want to prophesy new cars, money, houses and land. What about the danger of their souls as it relates to seeing Jesus. Think about it, O man or woman of God!

Chapter 15

Excuse Me Pastor, Are You Suffering from PMS?

When it comes to preachers and money, it is one of the most volatile subjects in the church in the United States. As I look at both sides of the argument, people sometimes want poor preachers while preachers want to live extravagant lives to avoid poverty or the appearance of poverty. To this day, many people still believe that preachers ought not to make a living off of the gospel. If a preacher starves, lives homeless, and can't provide for his or her family, it seems like a roar of approval is echoed without any tears of pity. It is part of the ministry. It goes with the territory.

The poorer preachers, the better, some may think. Then the opposite sentiment is also common: rich preachers with million-dollar mansions should go poor. Some pastors lust for high end cars, wives, women and an extra piece on the side. Yes, I am correct. There are preachers or pastors that have women on the side, as well as do other Christian believers. A preacher, if commanded by the Lord, is to live primarily off of the gospel of Jesus Christ, within the means of the legal definition of "reasonable compensation." Then people ought not to have a problem with it. But even if it were reasonable compensation, a small renegade bunch of folk will always have a problem with it. Then the question arises, "What is reasonable compensation?" It should not be a situation in which members of the local body are struggling and the pastors have major compensation from the church. Many of the members do not have money to pay their bills, buy food, or cannot afford reliable transportation to get from point "A to Z." There is fuel behind pastors who think they should have everything and the flock should have crumbs.

What is the fuel for these things? It is called PMS. That is, **Power, Money and Sex.** PMS is simply this from a medical standpoint since I have worked in the medical field for several years: Premenstrual (pree-MEN-struhl) syndrome (PMS) is a group of symptoms linked to the menstrual cycle. PMS symptoms occur one to two weeks before your period (menstruation or monthly bleeding starts). The symptoms usually go away after you start bleeding. PMS can affect menstruating women of any age and the effect is different for each woman. For some people, PMS is just a monthly bother. For others, it may be so severe that it makes it hard to even get through the day. PMS goes away when your monthly periods stop, such as when you get pregnant or go through menopause.

The causes of PMS are not clear, but several factors may be involved. Changes in hormones during the menstrual cycle seem to be an important cause. These changing hormone levels may affect some women more than others. Chemical changes in the brain may also be involved. Stress and emotional problems, such as depression, do not seem to cause PMS, but they may make it worse. Some other possible causes include: Low levels of vitamins and minerals, eating a lot of salty foods, which may cause you to retain (keep) fluid, drinking alcohol and caffeine, which may alter your mood and energy level. PMS often includes both physical and emotional symptoms, such as: acne, swollen or tender breasts, feeling tired, trouble sleeping, upset stomach, bloating, constipation, or diarrhea, headache or backaches, appetite changes or food cravings, joint or muscle pain, trouble with concentration or memory, tension, irritability, mood swings, or crying spells, and anxiety or depression. Symptoms vary from person to person.

Your doctor may diagnose PMS based on which symptoms you have, when they occur, and how much they affect your life. If you think you have PMS, keep track of which symptoms you have and how severe they are for a few months. A doctor will also want to make sure you do not have one of the following conditions that shares symptoms with PMS: Depression, anxiety menopause and, with men, andropause, Chronic fatigue syndrome (CFS), Irritable bowel syndrome (IBS), problems with the endocrine (EN-doh-kryn) system, which makes hormones.

There's a wide range of estimates regarding how many people suffer from PMS. Some doctors estimate that at least 85 percent of menstruating women and men have at least one PMS symptom as part of their routine cycle. Most of these people have fairly mild symptoms that do not need treatment. Others (about 3 to 8 percent) have a more severe form of PMS, called premenstrual dysphoric (dis-FOHR-ik) disorder (PMDD). PMS occurs more often in women who:

Are between their late 20s and early 40s

Have at least one child

Have a family history of depression

Have a past medical history of either postpartum depression or a mood disorder

Many things have been tried to ease the symptoms of PMS. No treatment works for every person. You may need to try different ones to see what works for you. Some treatment options include:

Lifestyle changes

Medications

Alternative therapies

Moreover, from the spiritual perspective, the Church and many pastors have PMS. The root cause is that some have allowed themselves to be drenched in this materialistic world.

In the United States, there are many of God's people and pastors that are wandering around aimless. Aimless means "without purpose or direction."

When you watch pastors get involved in questionable endeavors, it begs one to ask the question. What is our purpose and direction? The Head of the "Called Out Ones" gave us all the purpose and direction we need. In Matthew 28:18-20, the Great Commission is the current "standing orders" given to His apostles, prophets, evangelists, pastors, and teachers, for the perfecting or maturation of the saints, for the work of the service or ministry, for the edifying or building up of the edifice of the Body of Christ. This means that if we are not busy doing exactly what the Lord commissioned us to do and then we will do what the devil wants us to do. We will be busy doing everything else instead of what the Lord Jesus told us to do.

Therefore, a purposeless agenda is an agenda that obviously is unauthorized by the Lord and has no eternal value. However, there is also a purpose with intent using bits and pieces of the gospel given only as elements of truth to obscure the real agenda of duping the gullible saints according to Proverbs 14:15. With smooth words, the unsuspecting are told of obtaining great riches as a result of "sowing" money or goods into the man or woman of God.

There are many preachers in the United States that have built vast "empires," and there are many preachers that quietly go about their business without notice.

Yet, as they go about the business of the Father without notice, you will note that they are doing the most damage to the kingdom of darkness. Under the nose of the enemy, they are witnessing and testifying of the Lord and His gospel. People are getting into the Kingdom of God. In turn, they are introducing Jesus without fanfare and Broadway lights.

They are not distracted and they want to keep it that way. There are many preachers that want the notoriety and wish to be a part of the parade of the stars. The PMS Syndrome overthrows or consumes their every decision and desire. Yet, we see that when these things come, the expectation of their ministries and the person heading these ministries become the focal point of attention instead of them.

The Lord Jesus experienced "fame" when He came on the scene.

Matthew 4:24-25 says, "Then His fame went throughout all Syria; and they brought to Him all sick people who were afflicted with various diseases and torments, and those who were demon- possessed, epileptics, and paralytics; and He healed them. Great multitudes followed Him — from Galilee, and from Decapolis, Jerusalem, Judea, and beyond the Jordan."

The word "fame" means "heard." In other words, the people heard about Jesus. What we are seeing now is a perverted form of fame. People are no longer attracted to the holiness or righteousness that must be evident in the lives of pastors. People are attracted to the "bling" of preachers. The late Dr. Oral Roberts, in his autobiography that I read, said that the Lord told him not to chase after the "gold, the girls, or the glory." These days, you might as well add don't touch "the gentlemen."

In ministry, the glitter is litter. Kenneth Hagin's book is titled "The Midas Touch." It was a very prophetic book regarding the false teaching of the prosperity message. Just in case you don't understand what the "Midas Touch" means, it means "a king of Phrygia, who, according to one story, was given by Dionysus the power of turning everything he touched into gold." It also means as a phrase…. "The Midas Touch [is] the ability to make money out of anything one undertakes." The same is happening among some pastors today; they believe that everything that they touch must turn into gold. The push to be famous and rich in ministry is relentless.

Sadly, it seems like this is the only pursuit among some ministers today. This kind of perverted fame is evident in many sectors of the administration (see 1 Corinthians 12:5) of the Lord Jesus. We should not lose heart, because there are a few that will not chase after uncertain riches or minister for filthy lucre or illicit gain.

In 2 Corinthians 4:1-2, Paul said, "Therefore, since we have this ministry, as we have received mercy, we do not lose heart. But we have renounced the hidden things of shame, not walking in craftiness nor handling the Word of God deceitfully, but by manifestation of the truth commending ourselves to every man's conscience in the sight of God." Listen to the heart of Paul that is virtually absent in some of today's pastors: 1 Corinthians 9:11-18, *"Do I say these things as a mere man? Or does not the law say the same also? For it is written in the law of Moses, "You shall not muzzle an ox while it treads out the grain." Is it oxen God is concerned about? Or does He say it altogether for our sakes? For our sakes, no doubt, this is written, that he who plows should plow in hope, and he who threshes in hope should be partaker of his hope.*

If we have sown spiritual things for you, is it a great thing if we reap your material things? If others are partakers of this right over you, are we not even more? Nevertheless we have not used this right, but endure all things lest we hinder the gospel of Christ. Do you not know that those who minister the holy things eat of the things of the temple, and those who serve at the altar partake of the offerings of the altar? Even so the Lord has commanded that those who preach the gospel should live from the gospel.

But I have used none of these things, nor have I written these things that it should be done so to me; for it would be better for me to die than that anyone should make my boasting void. For if I preach the gospel, I have nothing to boast of, for necessity is laid upon me; yes, woe is me if I do not preach the gospel!

For if I do this willingly, I have a reward; but if against my will, I have been entrusted with a stewardship. What is my reward then? That when I preach the gospel, I may present the gospel of Christ without charge, that I may not abuse my authority in the gospel."

It's only in isolated places where you hear any preaching along these lines. Quite the opposite is preached because to preach anything else, it would not bring in the money. If you are not making money or turning everything that you do into something that will produce money, then you are not considered successful.

A home, cars, clothing, airplanes, large honorariums and book deals is a false measurement of success. Some pastors seek big buildings, big honorariums, and large groups of people to minister to, but forget to notice the distinguishing factor of the ministry of Jesus. The power of the Holy Spirit was upon the Lord Jesus to heal the sick, cast out devils, and heal other diseases. In other words, Jesus had the goods. The proof of His ministry was evident.

There is indisputable evidence of the ministry of Jesus but is there the same or similar evidence in pastors today? The Lord gives us the measurement that tells us that either we have the power of God or we don't. Notice what Jesus said in

Luke 12:48, "But he who did not know, yet committed things deserving of stripes, shall be beaten with few. For everyone to whom much is given, from him much will be required; and to whom much has been committed, of him they will ask the more."

You see, it is not about what you have and what you do not have as far as God's power is concerned. There is no sense going to a chicken restaurant if the chicken isn't good. Yet, we go to places where the power of God is nonexistent and there is a reason. First, there is no living out the Word of God. There may be preaching but there may not be any living of what is preached. The power of God never flows out because one says that there is power. The evidence is when the life of the person God uses is holy on the level that the Word requires.

Second, the power of God is not left to us to turn on and off when we want. The Holy Spirit is the One that administers the power of God as He wills, not as we will.

Third, all things done must point back to the Lord Jesus and the gospel that He commissioned us to preach. The release of the power of God serves as a witness to them to repent of their sins and believe on the Lord Jesus Christ to be saved.

We do not have to force the issue. We do not have to put ourselves out on a limb. We do not have to advertise. When the Holy Spirit sees fit that the Word is preached, that a person's life lines up with the Word, and the people are prepared to receive, it's all left up to the Holy Spirit, not us. God will not be put on the spot. He is God and not a genie. So people end up in places where there is a chance that God's power might show up. If you were to count on your hand how many times the Lord does something spectacular, you will shock yourself.

The gospel message is very simple, yet we have made it into something to force God to do something to prove something. God is God. He sits on the throne. He does as He pleases. He honors faith in His Word. God does not owe us anything. We owe Him all. So when it comes to power, money and sex, we need to ask ourselves a couple of questions. How long will it be until we come to our senses and be what He wants us to be instead of trying to make God be something that he already is? And when will we cry out for balance?

As unknown author once stated, *"Power, money and sex will not purchase happiness for the man who has no concept of what he wants; money will not give him a code of values, that is, if he's evaded the knowledge of what to value, and it will not provide him with a purpose, if he's evaded the choice of what to seek. Money will not buy intelligence for the fool, or admiration for the coward, or respect for the incompetent. The man who attempts to purchase the brains of his superiors to serve him, with his money replacing his judgment, ends up becoming the victim of his inferiors. The men of intelligence desert him, but the cheaters and the frauds come flocking to him, drawn by a law which he has not yet discovered: That no man may be smaller than his money. Is that the reason why you call it evil?"*

Our culture encourages people to reason and work their way through with goals for power, money and sex. Many exist to simply acquire power and possessions. This is represented in what they call 'the American dream' which may be summarized in the words "bigger and better." Also, in Europe, there is belief in endless progress so that technology may bring more and better. The progression of this is through mere human reasoning which is the primary focus in the Church.

Some Christians and pastors buy into this as much as unbelievers; indeed 'prosperity teaching' stems from the American dream rather than the New Testament. The general idea is that being a Christian makes your worldly expectations even more certain. This comes out of Scriptures confusing needs with materialistic wants. Some pastors infer that all Christians should be rich. This is often linked with pressure to line some pastors' pockets. Here the greatest danger is making money and possessions central so that they rule Christian lives.

In contrast, the focus of the Gospel changes the depths of your being through the love of God being poured out. In the kingdom of God things are different because here power, money and sex should be viewed as worthless compared to the lordship of Jesus Christ. Pivoting around money means that Christ is not central. Venerating (or having someone with superior authority) power or sex takes away worship which belongs to God. The very nature of the Gospel means that this world's values are not the scale to measure by. Christ gave himself on the cross so that by the power of the Holy Spirit Christians can have self-giving love. Christians should really ponder on the orientations and priorities which exist in church and personal life today. If all hinges on money then money has taken the place of Christ (so untrue). If anything has a greater priority than Christ himself then his lordship has been compromised. Living in a world which venerates sex, orientates around money, and lusts for power is no excuse for enthronement of these false gods among believers.

The ancient mistake of Simon Magnus, in Acts 8, was to try to buy spiritual gifts for cash, so they could be turned into money. Today, there are many modern parallels. As soon as you put a price tag on anything it is destroyed. This is because you are devaluing the holy and the eternal by rating God's gifts in terms of this corrupted temporary and dying age. We must learn afresh to draw a line between things which are and holy and that which is temporary and tainted. The false gods among the Lord's people must be dethroned. Where power, money and sex are venerated in Christian groups, this must be rooted out.

Power

Christian power in the New Testament is always in the flow of the Holy Spirit who brings the gospel to reality in Christians. Power conflicts arise when the Holy Spirit, working in terms of the gospel, is opposed by people who pivot on their own human thought and human effort.

Human power:

Human power is based on human reasoning.

Human power structures are built through human effort.

Human power tends to exploit.

Human power is often oppressive as in domination and manipulation.

Human power easily becomes corrupt.

Divine power

God brings people together at heart level.

His central thrust is self-giving love.

God's reasoning comes from His love.

God never dominates or manipulates.

God works through revelation which is at a higher level than human reasoning.

Manipulation is alien to the Spirit of God.

Dominating persons impose their own will rather than listening to God.

The authority of love wins your heart; in contrast, authority rooted in reason is often coercive. Both the fall and the temptation of Christ offered false reasoning as a route to illegitimate power. Both involved manipulation with a view to domination. Human weakness grasps at reasoning as a path to power while the divine man laid aside the legitimate power of his glory (Philippians 2:5-11).

Divine power is exercised relative to heart condition. Human power moves on the axis of control and/or self-interest. God could have so much control as to make every robot ever made to look wildly out of hand. Even so, the fact is that His central focus is on winning hearts and taming hearts, so God's activities relate not so much to time or to control but to heart condition. Christians do well to muse on their own heart condition. A stained heart creates an impasse to the Almighty. A broken or a wounded heart is something which he longs to heal and to restore. When God looks at a person he sees not so much their clothes or even their body but their hearts, which He longs to occupy because then He will have their body and clothes anyway.

Domination and manipulation in the church is particularly offensive to God because these practices have much more to do with the way evil forces operate. Fear of failure and anxiety about others being more able are common motives which fuel these bad practices. Leaders are failing when they resort to manipulation and domination. The sad fact is that this drives people from the church and some will even be driven from the faith. The end never justifies the means so we cannot do the Lord's work by using the methods of the opposition.

Domination is when someone tries to override your will by physical force or argument as in shouting. They aim to rule over your life in that matter. When domination is not possible, *manipulation* kicks in with bending and twisting. They try to get what they want by underhanded means such as lies and twisted information. Both domination and manipulation involve getting control over you without any right to do so.

Things would be very simple if only divine power operated in the church with the exclusion of all the murky dimensions of conflicting human power. The reality is one in which operates with the occasional intrusion of divine power. In revival, human power has to be minimized to make space for God's power to be made known. The balance can sometimes be on a knife edge because a power vacuum creates instability and the opportunity for chaos. Proper balance preserves what God is doing without leaving empty space for those who wish to impose their own agenda.

Money

When we think of idols we expect something to look at in terms of a face or some kind of form. However, what really makes the thing an idol is the ideas around the image. The Euro was created by human beings with a particular value and a given image for the purpose of trade and banking. The folly is in forgetting this human origin and using money to define life. The same is true for the pound and other currency, although the Euro is very new so the 'forgetting' has been fast. Now money defines us in terms of how much an hour we may earn and the value of our possessions. The 'forgetting' has overlooked our value in the eyes of God and chosen to embrace an idol made by human minds to assess people, enterprise and governments. The balance sheet stands supreme to dehumanize people and give false evaluation to all human activity.

When Jesus spoke about serving mammon or money (Matthew 6:24 and 16:9-13) He was using a term of the day which symbolized honor to wealth and acquisition, as if it was a person. So He laid on the line a straight choice between serving God or worshipping wealth and acquisition. How unfortunate that the impression is given today in many churches and Christian organizations that money is a "so called" solution to most problems. This comes from the reasoning of our age in which money is a god; and the Christian church should expose the lie, especially among the Lord's people.

Currently, the exaltation of money in the Christian church is doing great damage because there is widespread belief that any kind of progress depends on accumulation of wealth and acquisition. Some pastors even infer a connection between the greatness of a person's faith and a person's material possessions. How unfortunate that by this measure Jesus would be at the bottom of the league with Paul close behind! Confusion has combined rationalization about money making, and 'faith,' which may be more in money than in Jesus. There is an enormous difference between simple faith in Jesus to provide for needs, and techniques of 'faith' for getting rich.

The currency of the Kingdom of God is hearts filled with the love of Christ and in China that is what they spend in evangelism. In the West, to the extent that the church builds from a love affair with wealth and acquisition, then God is alienated, people are scattered and things fall apart anyway. Collapse often happens naturally although God loves His people enough to even induce collapse when necessary, because they need reminding that only one God reigns.

Flirting with money takes many forms. Here are some provocative questions. In your Christian organization how does time spent in financial planning compare with time spent in prayer? What is the first thing mentioned when there is a new project? Does the committee lie in bed awake at night worrying most about the strength of the prayer meeting or the balance sheet? Are Christians depersonalized into cash machines for leadership projects with milking on a weekly basis? Is investment primarily in people or in property?

The violence of mammon is in the destruction of the true worth of a child of Christ. Money also decimates or reduces to non-existence fellowship by supplanting it with financial consciousness intruding into the space which should be the Lord's. Even a marginal drift can bring ruin. Read the Old Testament to see how the people of God courted ruin by installing false gods beside the Lord. Idolatry is the attempt to manipulate by introducing false gods into places which belong to the Lord.

Christian values are based on Jesus. The Christian value for persons comes from their creation in the image of God, and their dynamic fellowship with the Lord through the personal indwelling of the Holy Spirit of God. This is far above the limits of reasoning in balance sheets because the currency of Christian values is the love of Christ. This has no connection at all with human currency. The pound, the euro, the dollar, and every other currency are many leagues below the true values in the gospel. The Christian Church is the vanguard in revaluing humanity by bringing a return to Christ in the gospel. This will be ruined if the church has a tongue in cheek heart-throb for wealth and acquisition. Love for Christ should not be defiled by flirting with money.

Sex

Sexuality is a fundamental part of being human that you cannot remove from our existence. Throughout history there have been people who have tried to conceal and repress their sexuality although this has always led to complications and frequently to disaster. Even in childhood gender is an important part of who we are. As with every other gift from God, sexuality can be used positively or be corrupted so as to have all kinds of negative effects. The Bible teaches that God created sexuality and has given us a framework in which human sexuality can be handled positively.

Faithfulness in marriage (and courtship) is a reflection of God's faithfulness in the gospel. The faithfulness of God in persisting with building relationships with people through the cross is reflected in human faithfulness as shown in families, friendships and marriage. Faithfulness breeds security and trust so that relationships not only stick but become stronger. The proper setting of sex is as part of faithfulness in marriage. The Bible teaches that this physical union is so profound as to extend into a spiritual union which is why using prostitutes pollutes deep inside the human spirit (1 Corinthians 6:12-20). This denial of the faithfulness of God destroys not only within the participant but in all their contacts, as trust is undermined and all the best things in life become tainted.

Sexual union was designed by God to further cement the loving relationship of marriage. In this context, sex is a unifying component within the many facets of good marriage relationships. If sex is separated from marriage, then the physical act is isolated without the checks and balances of a loving relationship. Out of the context of marriage sex becomes addictive in a very harmful way. Progress of this addiction craves more sensation and so pushes into greater promiscuity and may be followed by perversions and the use of drugs to heighten sensation. This wreaks havoc in a person's character. Ability to trust in personal relationships is devastated. Loneliness and isolation increase and character defects, which may have started the process, in the first place, become compounded and far more complicated.

Forgiveness through the gospel of Jesus Christ is wonderful, because this happens with the presence of the Holy Spirit to cleanse and rebuild our characters as life progresses. There is something rather cruel about presenting the gospel as merely forgiveness without the power of the Holy Spirit being invited to address the inner problems which feed our disposition to sin in the first place. If we are to have strong Christians who can resist the seduction of the age in which we live, then the continual activity of the Holy Spirit in building Christian character is essential.

The reason that is so famously unsuccessful in controlling sexuality is that words and argument carry limited weight against the passions of the human heart. Where Christian fellowships have moved away from deep spirituality and engaged in a more mind-centered Christianity then the power to stand strong sexually is limited. There is nothing like the inner presence and free working of the Holy Spirit of God for promoting good judgment in relationships of every kind. The power within can deal with flooding temptation although mere rules and information fold easily.

We cannot separate the deep human need to be wanted, or each person's longing for significance, from sexuality. Unfortunately, broken-heartedness often looks for comfort in the wrong places. Sex promises instant gratification, along with an illusion that it will solve problems across the board. After those few minutes of emotional comfort and physical sensation, little consolation remains from what in reality was the compounding of your problems. The false logic of what we want to believe can lead easily to sex outside of marriage, although afterwards the harsh reality of deep complications bounces back. It does not matter if nobody else on earth knows, because immorality extends our own inner disjuncture, as well as fragmenting our relationship with God.

The idea of maximizing pleasure is very strong in our society. Christian faith certainly brings pleasure but only as a byproduct of a personal relationship with Jesus Christ. The modern world is obsessed with pleasure, which it idolizes through hunting down as many different ways as possible of releasing endorphins in the brain. Many Christians never question the idea of 'pleasure comes first.' We must beware of following this pressure to put pleasure in the center of our lives. Pleasure cannot be installed where God belongs and must never be treated like God. This includes sexual pleasure. In the proper context, be that simply pleasant company or something deeper, there is no harm. The harm comes in desire to take that which is not ours to have, which is lust.

The natural thing to do is to cloke lust under some more noble cover. Some women know that the seducer and the spouse both say, "I love you!" so a better cloak is needed. 'Fate' is often used, especially in films, where the argument for adultery is often, "Fate has put us together." or "We were destined to be together." The truth is that, never mind fate, there has been some very human hoping, dreaming and conniving going on. Occasionally, Christians are so foolish as to say their action is "God's will" when, in fact, it flies in the face of the faithfulness of God and what the Bible says about sex. James has an explanation that makes more sense, *"Then, after desire has conceived, it gives birth to sin; and sin, when it is full-grown, gives birth to death"* (James 1:15 NIV).

The age in which we live is seductive in every sense of the word. Every kind of promise tries to seduce us to love the goods and experiences on offer. Deception of every kind abounds, from exaggerated adverts, to love songs which deceive us into thinking that immorality will heal our broken hearts. The truth is that fornication and adultery break hearts. The modern age preys on inner emptiness and loneliness. Sexual seduction is just one of many seductions in the modern age which combine together to break down resistance and weaken resolve. Seduction is particularly successful in our age when your inner emptiness is linked with the false assumption that sex brings instant fulfillment which will last. Today, when someone sets out to sexually seduce another person they have a relatively easy job because everyone has been plied with a whole range of false values already.

Christians are most at risk when their existence is centered on reasons and arguments rather than openness to the long term effect of the Holy Spirit of God on their character. The drift toward mind oriented 'faith' leaves voids which can be exploited. Deception is easy if it connects with misdirected heart longings. False promises are especially attractive when you want to believe them anyway. This is the world in which immorality is equated with love and 'me first' indulgence is legitimized despite the ruin brought to families and marriages. Today Christians often lack inner strength built up by the presence of the Holy Spirit, so many are highly susceptible to the mixture of flattery, deception, indulgence and sensation.

Sex as the revered idol is disarmed of power by exposure of its lies through confrontation with the cross of Christ. The removes guilt and recreates the spirits of those broken by the violence of this false god. results in isolation, illegitimacy, and reduced self-worth. This devalues both sexes, breaks down marriages and fragments families. Only the gospel can break open the prison of 'adulthood' with its lie of 'liberation' so that the reality of isolation, shame and guilt can be transformed again into proper relationships through the power of the Holy Spirit. The folly of putting pleasure first is corrected by the truth of a loving relationship in Christ Jesus, which is the only sure foundation for everlasting pleasure. However, pleasure (including sexual pleasure) is always secondary and comes out of your relationship with God and others.

Chapter 16

Excuse Me Pastor, Are You Addicted to Porn?

Confess to one another therefore your faults (your slips, your false steps, your offenses, your sins) and pray [also] for one another, that you may be healed and restored [to a spiritual tone of mind and heart]. The earnest (heartfelt, continued) prayer of a righteous man makes tremendous power available [dynamic in its working] (James 5:16 AMP).

One of my pastor friends told me he was addicted to porn. He woke me up in the middle of the night and realized I wasn't in bed. He stated, "I knew you would be up and I needed someone to talk to. I am here watching it right now to get my mind off the divorce that I went through." He walked into the living room and as soon as he called me, I heard the sounds of pornographic activity. He quickly changed the channel.

I began to question him as to what really brought him to that point. He stated, "My wife is gone and I do not want my church to know that I have this side to me." I quickly began to pray in mind as he was talking to me. Because I knew spirits beget other spirits and prey on the psyche of the person and soon you find yourself doing the thing that was on TV. Then he asked me, "Do you struggle with lust and pornography?" The more he asked the question, the more intense the conversation became. I was real with him. I told him, "That is not my thorn, but I do struggle with other things such as food, sex, and shopping. However, I have never been addicted to porn. I further explained that struggling with something is different from being addicted to something.

An addiction must have marked signs and symptoms and a morbid process that places a person's life in danger. Some say that pornography is not an addiction, but an Obsessive Compulsive Disorder (OCD). Although this definition is very thorough, pornography has environmental stressors which also demonstrate signs and symptoms that the person has lost control and possesses a morbid place of danger. But I reassured him that there is help both spiritually and medically before harm totally damages his life.

He later told me why his wife left him: because of what he wanted her to do sexually—acts to which she did not agree. It had been over twenty years of addiction and he'd hidden many porno DVDs from her. She could not take it any longer so she left him in the house and he did not know what to do. He would argue with her about what she saw: "I convinced her that I did not struggle with porn or lust. She had nothing to worry about." But he was lying.

I did not know it at the time; but that night was the first of many opportunities he had over the first ten years of the marriage to be honest about his porn addiction.

He stated to me that he was a pastor and pastors don't struggle with lust or porn. At least, no other pastor he knew struggled with it. He felt all alone.

The truth was he was not alone. I had friends he could have talked to. I could have gotten him some help before it reached that point in his life. He also had some other friends he lied to as well. He had other pastors he blew off when asked about sexual sins and struggles. In his mind, his intentions were good. He was trying to protect his marriage. The reality is, porn was telling him lies and he was buying right into them.

For the number of people who struggle with this, we do not talk about it quite enough. We do not talk about it in our families. We do not talk about it in our churches. We think avoiding it will make it go away. Statistically speaking, over 50 percent of the men reading this book have had exposure to pornography recently. And it's not just a "man's problem," either. About 30 percent of porn users online are women. It isn't going away.

No matter how many times you have looked at pornography, that was your 'last time.' Because you truly believe it is your last time buying the magazine, going to the web site, downloading the movies—you do not need to confess it, because it was the last time most, people say. Until tomorrow or next week or next month, it is the last time—until the next time. If porn can convince you that "this time is the last time," you'll never tell anyone.

You know what pornography has done to other marriages, to other friends, to other families, to other church leaders…but you are not really "addicted" to pornography. You can stop anytime you want. Besides it does not have the same effect on you that it does on other people. But it is hurting your life, your marriage, your kids, your church; your ministry like it has other people. You are in control of porn; it does not have to control you.

Porn wants you to live in secret. Porn causes us to weigh the cost of confessing against the cost of hiding and convinces us that hiding will be less painful. You think you are helping yourself and your marriage by hiding your porn addiction. Your wife—or husband—will not understand. It tells you that your marriage will not recover. Your credibility will not be able to be rebuilt.

Something I've learned the hard way: Hiding sin never provides us with the power to overcome it. The freedom you long for is found in confession. Freedom costs something up front, but not as much as bondage costs over time.

Believing these lies will never give you the power to overcome them. Trying to quit will not give you the power to quit. But freedom is possible. Here is what I believe with all of my heart: If you struggle with pornography, God isn't disappointed in you; He is fighting for you. He died and conquered sin and death so you can have victory in this area of your life.

Where do we begin? How can we overcome something that grips our hearts and keeps us living in shame and guilt? The first place I suggest everyone that struggles with pornography should start is with a Christian counselor. Some people need someone with greater perspective and wisdom than we have to help us overcome this struggle in our lives.

Beyond that, I want to share one principle with you that I believe has power to bring freedom, hope and healing to your heart. It will not be easy, but it will be worth it.

Healing comes through confession and prayer. The Bible says confess your faults one to another (I know that sounds very churchy, but take a look at this

Scripture: "Therefore confess your sins to each other and pray for each other so that you may be healed. The prayer of a righteous person is powerful and effective (James 5:16). "

The type of confession that James is talking about isn't a confession for forgiveness; it is confession for healing. There is a healing that comes to our hearts as we confess our sins with one another. Most of us have the "forgiveness" part of confession down. We know that in order to get forgiveness from God, we have to confess our sins. Maybe you grew up confessing to a priest, maybe it is something that you do in your quiet time with God, and maybe it is something that you do after you've made a huge mistake. Most of us know that forgiveness from God comes through confession.

We don't talk about the "healing" type of confession in the Church very often. In fact, we have built a religious system that tries to find healing through hiding our sins, and not confessing them. The sins we do confess are "safe" sins: bitterness, jealousy, materialism, anger and selfishness.

Some people are masters at this method. My friend appeared "authentic" for confessing socially acceptable sins while he lived as a prisoner to sins he was not willing to confess. For years, he forfeited the healing that God longed to bring to his heart not because he did not confess his sins to God, but because he refused to confess them to others that could also provide the help needed. Below are some truths that pornography can impact when it is brought to light:

Some Truths Porn Will Never Tell You

Temptation loses its power when we confess it.

Sin loses its ability to keep us fractured when it also is made known.

Addictions lose the control they have in our lives when confessed.

The secret sin you keep only has power as it remains a secret.

The light will always overcome darkness.

The difficult decision we face is to allow spiritual light into the darkest and most embarrassing parts of our heart.

God cannot heal the parts of our heart we refuse to bring into spiritual light. But when we do, we can be healed.

Chapter 17

Excuse Me Pastor, Do You Want Money or Ministry?

"Let the elders who perform the duties of their office well be considered doubly worthy of honor [and of adequate financial support, especially those who labor faithfully in preaching and teaching. For the Scripture says, You shall not muzzle an ox when it is treading out the grain, and again, The laborer is worthy of his hire" (I Timothy 5: 17-18) AMP.

Money and ministry or should I say, ministry and money, that is the question that should be addressed? I found myself in a quandary when I saw the recent episodes of the "Preachers of LA" and various ministers with whom I come in contact. It seems to be that of money first and no ministry. What a shame! Lavish-looking clothing nestled within the fine houses, some mega-churches with ornate pews, crystal chandeliers, and cushioned lifestyles when members of their own congregation are starving and have barely enough money to pay their own bills.

According to an article written by **Antwuan Malone**, <u>Candid Christianity</u>, "There is either too much, or not enough. The often polarizing issue of pastors and pay is usually a product of off-base perceptions of the church. People, who have problems with full-time, staffed pastors, most likely see the church as a profit organization that competes for your dollar over the church down the road.

Unfortunately, they aren't too far off. Many churches operate like corporations, with budget goals of gaining membership, in order to get money, to build bigger stuff, and gain more membership and get more stuff... etc. I've written about how for the good of God's people and the community. It's only reasonable to expect cynicism about profit when your budget model is designed to profit. If churches change the way they deal with money, it would go a long way toward changing the perception of "career" pastors.

Often, the amount of work God has for His leaders goes unseen, and often unaccounted for. People only see Sunday and assume pastors lie in bed most of the week, with maybe a few hours of study here and there. And heaven forbid he drive a nice car, or go on vacation to the islands.

Pastors have their part to play here as well. While being an effective pastor is a full time commitment, they must also guard against the temptations that come with the territory — namely greed, pride, and slothfulness. There is always work to be done, always ways God is speaking and moving in the lives of a congregation. No sooner does a pastor slow down to start indulging himself in the Me-Monster-Machine that has become "church," when the enemy attacks. Besides, true caring for people starts with being available in their darkest hours (which could be any time of the day or night). Even full time ministers have issues with being there for all members, but that only serves my point. People need pastors.

Some work on Sunday morning is probably the smallest percentage of their weekly efforts. Proper preparation for

God's Word, learning how to best identify the needs of the church and the unchurched, and researching, praying and hearing from God on how to address those needs are all time consuming tasks — too big for any margin. Part-time pastoring leaves much to be desired. It can be (and often is) done, but the ministry often suffers (or even the minister).

There is biblical precedence both for a man of God being cared for by a body of believers (the high priests, Timothy, for example), and for a man of God making it on his own without such provision (like many of the prophets, Paul, John the Baptist, even Jesus). The result really is that there is no cookie cutter solution.

Even with the money. We have to be careful with telling God how he will take care of His own. He has shown that He can ordain either scenario.

I totally agree with Mr. Antwuan Malone in the aforementioned statements. However, it goes deeper than what he wrote. I remember being part of a start-up ministry and the local church was flourishing. As time went along, people started to leave because it was more about the pastor and money than ministry and people. I remember one of our meetings when I looked at the financial report. Eighty percent of the money was going to the pastor for his $289,000 home, payment for the car, gas for the car, cell phone, payments for life insurance that will pay off any of his debts if he were to meet his demise before his wife, travel expenses, laptop, internet and even funding love offerings during the worship service, for that would fatten his pockets for ancillary things that he needed. However, he was not using these things to benefit the local body that he served or really the Body of Christ. Many of the members often talked about this, but there was no one to utter a complaint since he started that ministry.

I know, as the above Scripture mentions, we should take care of our pastors; but I do not think that the pastors should take advantage of the body, knowing that people in the church have barely enough to pay their own bills. And besides, there was no money left in the budget for ministry. I looked closer because I knew that three-fourths of the music ministry staff left because of this one statement he made…. "You will not get paid until I get my money." What a tragedy!

This man had a great job at a Fortune 500 company and in upper level management but his main purpose was to design and craft that local church because he was fired. This is sad indictment for a so called "man of God" to take advantage of the church in that manner. He would preach sermons that would make you jump out of your seat and sometimes say, "We will not be here long today," because he had personal things to do. To me, he viewed his position as a lazy pastor that only wanted money for him and no ministry. He eventually got a job for health insurance reasons, but he was really lazy.

There was also an incident in which a young lady consulted with him privately and told him about her personal life. He leaked the information in pillow talk with his wife which exacerbated the conversation throughout the entire church. Later, she left the church to go to school and better her life, but tragedy hit her once again. She called him and explained to him that her mother who was in the nursing home had passed and she needed help for funeral expenses. He was not man enough to call her and to express his sympathy or empathy because he lost one of his parents as well. He sent the head deacons out to tell her that since she had moved away from the church that the church could not help her, but at the same time a plea came from him to ask each member in the church to give $1 or more for one of his members who had a mentally challenged child and the money would go to pay for her private schooling.

He could have used a similar plea for the young lady and sent the money to the funeral home to make sure that everything was covered. Is not that what church is for to help those who are in need? It caused me to be stifled in my thoughts about his calling as a minister and pastor and I could not sit under his leadership because he was so egocentric, instead of looking out for those who were in need.

Although the young lady was no longer at that church, she was faithful when she was there and he could have taken that into consideration, but it was all about him and the pillow talks at home that prevented her from getting her mother buried properly. The young lady went into the hospital after that because she became suicidal. Her mother was buried by the State of Alabama, where they take the bodies of all people who do not have insurance, throw the bodies into the ground, and cover them with dirt. There is no real vault or metal casket, but a box that they put them in after they have been embalmed, and she did not even see her mother buried because she had no proper help.

The question that I am posing is this: "Do you think personal vendettas should take place as in the above ministry?" My answer is NO! We are all here to help each other. Excuse me pastor, I don't want to be part of your church? And I highlight this because real ministry focuses on the Kingdom of God mentioned in Romans 14: 17 (Righteousness, Peace and Joy in Holy Ghost). Where is the righteousness, peace and joy in the Holy Ghost for a pastor to treat God's creation like that when the pastor did not create the people themselves? I sometimes question the integrity of many of the pastors who say that are called to pastor a church but the whole ploy is to satisfy their own proclivity.

When Is Enough Money Enough

I read on Pastor Chuck Swindoll's blog in 2008 entitled <u>Pastoral Traps: Greed</u> in which he stated, "We can easily fall into the trap of money-grubbing." Or in simpler terms, we can be greedy.

This is true if money winds up in the pastor's pocket that was earmarked for some other realm of ministry. This is true if the minister is asked about his financial policy with regard to ministry money, and he responds with a "that's-none-of-your-business" type of reaction. Dependable shepherds are not motivated by what Peter referred to as "sordid gain" (1 Peter 5:2). The old King James Version bluntly calls it "filthy lucre." That's an archaic expression, but it says it straight. "Not for filthy lucre, but of a ready mind."

My counsel to all pastors is to keep your hands out of the money, period! Don't give change. Don't take up the offerings. Don't count the offering . . . or even concern yourself with where the money is counted. And by all means, don't try to find out who gives the most! If you do, it will affect the way you preach.

We pastors have to beware carrying out ministry just for the money or officiating at a wedding, for example, because there's money in it, or doing a funeral because you'll get a hundred bucks. Greed has no shame. It will wink at you and tempt you, especially in a day when many pastors are underpaid relative to their education.

What I'm saying has nothing to do with "muzzling the ox." My warning is simple: If you're not careful, you'll find yourself justifying greed. Please . . . don't go there."

I really agree with Dr. Swindoll's statements. It places pastors in the vein of "Money hungry pastors" and not "Ministry minded leaders." When money becomes the reason for your preaching, I do believe that the pastor needs to resign. That is a strong statement for me to make but it is true. I know we all have thorns but our personal thorns should not be at the expense of the little old grandmothers, single parents, abused mothers, fathers, children and other family members who do not have food to eat. In other words it takes away from the central focus of who Jesus is really about and nullifies Matthew 28: 19-20, "Go then and make disciples of all the nations, baptizing them into the name of the Father and of the Son and of the Holy Spirit, teaching them to observe everything that I have commanded you, and behold, I am with you all the days (perpetually, uniformly, and on every occasion), to the [very] close *and* consummation of the age. *Amen (so let it be).*

I was teaching Sunday school teachers one Wednesday night and the subject was "Welcoming All People." After I got through teaching, my pastor made a comment, "He stated that we should have the word "GO" printed on inside and out of the vestibule area to remind us to spread the gospel. The lesson was on the Parable of the Great Supper out of Luke 14:7-24 AMP). I will only print the portion that pastor was alluding to.

It stated, *"But Jesus said to him, A man was once giving a great supper and invited many; And at the hour for the supper he sent his servant to say to those who had been invited, Come, for all is now ready. But they all alike began to make excuses and to beg off. The first said to him, I have bought a piece of land, and I have to go out and see it; I beg you, have me excused. And another said, I have bought five yoke of oxen, and I am going to examine and put my approval on them; I beg you, have me excused. And another said, I have married a wife, and because of this I am unable to come. So the servant came and reported these [answers] to his master. Then the master of the house said in wrath to his servant, Go quickly into the great streets and the small streets of the city and bring in here the poor and the disabled and the blind and the lame. And the servant [returning] said, Sir, what you have commanded me to do has been done, and yet there is room. Then the master said to the servant, Go out into the highways and hedges and urge and constrain [them] to yield and come in, so that my house may be filled. For I tell you, not one of those who were invited shall taste my supper."*

You can clearly see the excuses of those who did not want to come, but the word(s) *Go*, or *Go quickly* really stood out. That is our mandate. I know the church has bills and other things that money is needed for, but the main job for us as Christians and pastor is not to be bothered with how much money people give in their tithes, but if we seek ye first the Kingdom of God and His righteousness, all these other things will be added unto us (Matthew 6:33). I think many of us as leaders and pastors have it backwards, and that is why people are not being saved or coming to the local church.

Chapter 18

Excuse Me Pastor, I Can't Come to Your Church Because I Am Gay!

"Know ye not that the unrighteous shall not inherit the kingdom of God? Be not deceived; neither fornicators, nor idolaters, nor adulterers, nor effeminate, nor abusers of themselves with mankind, nor thieves, nor covetous, nor drunkards, nor revilers, nor extortioners, shall inherit the kingdom of God. And such were some of you (1 Corinthians 6:9-11)."

One of my friends who is very rooted in the Word of God, and was first a highly thought of teacher and preacher in another denomination, left there because of the error in teaching and became a Christian. But to his dismay, it was not much different when he became part of Christian Church since he was gay. Pastors would get up and dog homosexuals out verbally but he began to see the pastors were hungry for what he calls *"His Gay Money."* I wondered why he stopped attending church and he stated, "I know there is no perfect local church body, but these pastors and preachers are the same ones that I would meet at the clubs and some would even ask me home to have sexual encounters with them, but I refused."

These acts left a bitter taste in his mouth so he started listening and streaming on the internet to people like Joel Osteen who spoke of love and the Kingdom of God. I tried to get him to go to church with me, but in the back of his mind, "The Love factor of all God's creation was not being taught locally." He stated most of the pastors, deacons and choir members that he saw at the church were the same ones at the clubs and wanted to take him home. This shattered his view of the Christian Church. He stated, "Why should I be part of something that the pastors of these local churches are doing themselves and, by the way, I did not ask to be gay or homosexual, this fell as my lot. I prayed and prayed that God would take it away from me, but the thorn still remained." He further stated, "I know that I am a Christian," and told me that I showed him more love than any pastor or church could ever show him. He went on to say that the some of the pastors of the churches are very prejudicial due to their fear and ignorance of not understanding that all gay men do not want every man they see. Furthermore, some pastors (gay or straight) do not show Christ-like love. That was the reason he does not trust some pastors or some straight men. He and I go out to movies, talk about church related issues (which still makes him upset), but most of all He is still my friend.

I read a three page (3) article by Corey Dade, that I must place in this book which describes the complexity of gays in the black church or in the Church Universal called, *Blacks, Gays And The Church: A Complex Relationship*. He states, *"Fairly or not, African-Americans have become the public face of resistance to same-sex marriage, owing to their religious beliefs and the outspoken opposition of many black pastors. Yet the presence of gays and lesbians in black churches is common. And the fact that they often hold leadership positions in their congregations is the worst kept secret in black America. While many black pastors condemn gays and lesbians from the pulpit, and the choir lofts behind them often are filled with gay singers and musicians. Some male pastors themselves have been entangled in scandals involving alleged affairs with men. "Persons who are in the closet serve on the deacon boards, serve in the ministry, serve in every capacity in the church," the Rev. Dennis W. Wiley, pastor of Covenant Baptist United Church of Christ in Maryland, says of black churches. Wiley is a prominent advocate of gay marriage. "I do believe certain hypocrisy is there."*

President Obama's recent announcement that he supports same-sex marriage turned the spotlight on about gay rights. Most polls show African-Americans evenly divided about gay marriage, but the vocal opposition, led by preachers, has gained more attention.

"This particular decision I find appalling, and I could not disagree with the president more on it," the Rev. Patrick Wooden, senior pastor of the Upper Room Church of God in Christ in North Carolina, said on . Wooden helped lead the recent campaign that outlawed gay marriage in his state.

Last week, the National Association for the Advancement of Colored People (NAACP) passed a endorsing same-sex marriage as a civil right to be protected by the U.S. Constitution.

Churches Reap Benefits

Some say pastors' hostility cuts hard against the history of how countless black churches have flourished. The virtuosity of gay singers, musicians and composers has been the driving force in developing popular gospel choirs — even chart-topping, Grammy-winning acts — that make money for a church, help expand congregations and raise the profiles of pastors.

It all happens under an unspoken "don't ask, don't tell" custom that allows gay people to be active in the church, though closeted, and churches to reap the benefits of their membership. Some say the arrangement is not only hypocritical, but exploitative. "On the one hand, you're nurtured in the choir but you also have to sit through some of those fire and brimstone sermons about homosexuality being an abomination," says E. Patrick Johnson, an openly gay gospel singer and author of **<u>Sweet Tea: An Oral History of Black Gay Men of the South</u>**, *"But a lot of these choirs or choir directors, or ministers of music, will not be open about their sexuality for fear of repercussion from their pastors and church members, but they allow the church to exploit their talent," says Johnson, also a Northwestern University professor whose expertise includes black studies and sexuality. Johnson and others believe that modern gospel music itself is largely defined by the artistry of black gay men.*

Bishop Yvette Flunder of Oakland, Calif., is openly gay and the founder of The City of Refuge UCC in 1991 and pro-gay black pastor openly welcomes lesbian, gay, bisexual and transgender members. Flunder once said during a 2010 that gospel choirs "always" have been havens for LGBT people: "In our indigenous expression, that wasn't a problem. It was Christianity that demonized gay people."

As Johnson puts it, "You can't throw a shoe back through history without hitting gay and lesbian women and even transgender singers. "Johnson describes church choirs as a welcoming community within a community "where you meet other gay people, so it becomes a form of socializing."

Commentator Keith Boykin, who is African-American and gay, calls it a paradox: "The church might be the most homophobic and most homointolerant of any institution in the black community."

Wooden, the pastor in North Carolina, agrees that the presence of gays and lesbians in choirs or other church ministries reveals the "duplicity and frankly, the hypocrisy of the black church... The thing that troubles me is these people are almost taken advantage of. As long as they can sing, people look the other way."

However, Wooden insists "we are not all homophobic." He says he welcomes members of the LGBT community to worship at his church. He says his church also has continued to support gay members who have contracted HIV/AIDS, unlike some other churches that ostracize them — a practice many people on both sides of the issue say has been common.

But that's where Wooden's self-described sense of fairness ends. He forbids LGBT people from participating in the choir or any other church ministries.

"If you love them — truly love them — you will tell them the truth on the front side," Wooden says. "We believe homosexuality is a sin. Those who serve, you want their lifestyles to uphold the standards of the church. This is not limited to homosexuals or lesbians. If I know an individual is committing adultery or living with a member of the opposite sex who they're not married to, they can't serve either."

I remember a story at our local church where a transgender female came and was arrayed in clothing like that of a woman. Many of the members began to utter comments and she felt and heard them as well. She never came back. Mind you, she had come several times before, but I told my Sunday school class, "Do not put your mouth on the person. It is God that will do the separating and not us."

It was so embarrassing, even the pastor made jokes after the service about how she was dressed even better than his wife---the so called "First Lady." This terminology is a phrase of the world and not biblically based. This term can mean two things to the church proper: (1) there must be a second lady somewhere or it may be (2) the first lady that walks into the local church for the day. Excuse me, pastor, what a church mess we place ourselves into.

Consequences, Whether Closeted or Out

A small but growing number of churches, such as the Rev. Wiley's and Flunder's City of Refuge United Church of Christ, publicly welcome LGBT members, and their ranks are swelling with people leaving intolerant churches.

But many others say they are torn between their allegiance to their churches, which form the cultural and institutional backbone of black communities, and their desire to live free of homophobia. They often choose the former, convinced that their sexuality is a sin.

"They would rather suppress their identity than denounce their church," says Sharon J. Lettman-Hicks, executive director of the National Black Justice Coalition, an LGBT advocacy group. "I've seen people refuse to divorce themselves from their church in spite

of the ignorance that spews from the pulpit. ... It's their way of repenting. They victimize themselves through self-oppression."

Gospel music superstar and mega-church pastor, Donnie McClurkin, shocked the non-gospel world years ago by revealing in a 2001 book that God "delivered" him from a gay "lifestyle" that he said was a result of being sexually abused as a boy.

McClurkin, who has said being gay is a choice, was criticized by the gay community for setting back the LGBT goal of gaining acceptance.

When gospel music star, Tonex (Anthony Charles Williams II), came out in 2009, the gospel music world turned on him, and his record sales plummeted. He left his family church, where he'd been a pastor, and reinvented himself as , now a favorite in the LGBT music scene.

Rise of Black Homophobia: Morality Turns Political

For decades, black ministers addressed LGBT people in their sermons only occasionally. This was true even as HIV/AIDS began claiming the lives of numerous African-American men in black churches, especially gospel singers in the early 1990s.

By 2004, a number of high-profile black ministers emerged as outspoken opponents of same-sex marriage as part of their alignment with the conservative Christian movement, which helped re-elect President George W. Bush that year. Black ministers and black lawmakers helped pass gay marriage bans in several states. In exchange, ministers received federal funds for their community programs through Bush's faith-based initiative.

In 2006, the National Black Justice Coalition held its first Black Church Summit in Atlanta, at which the Rev. Al Sharpton became the highest-profile pastor to denounce homophobia and call for greater inclusion of LGBT people.

Pastors No Strangers to Gay Sex Scandals

The sexual behavior of some male pastors, many of them also gospel singers, also has stoked rumors or led to scandal. Bishop Eddie Long, the leader of one of the nation's largest black churches, in suburban Atlanta, was sued in 2010 by three young men who claimed Long coerced them into sexual relationships. Long denied the accusations and the cases were settled out of court.

The controversy was all the more notable because Long was a prominent supporter of Georgia's gay marriage ban, passed in 2004, and a proposed U.S. constitutional ban. He rankled many civil rights veterans when he and the Rev. Bernice King, a daughter of Martin Luther King Jr. and Coretta Scott King (who supported gay marriage), led a march to protest same-sex marriage that started at the King family crypt. "Some of my colleagues protest too greatly," Wiley says.

Prior to the accusations against Long, most controversies rarely escaped mention inside black communities and gospel music circles.

The Bay Area in the 1970s had arguably the most visible presence of LGBT members in black churches, just as the broader gay rights movement had gained momentum in the region. The Love Center Church in Oakland, Calif., founded by the late Bishop Walter Hawkins, one of gospel music's biggest stars in the 1970s and 1980s, made waves for welcoming black gays and lesbians.

Following the 1991 death of the Rev. James Cleveland, the gospel music legend still regarded as the "King" of the genre, a male member of Cleveland's choir sued his estate claiming that he contracted HIV due to his with the singing icon. The lawsuit was settled out of court."

As stated in I Corinthians (listed above) dissects this in his book, <u>*Gay Christian Survivors: Defeating Anti-Gay Views With The Word of God*</u> *states "The Scripture also uses the word "effeminate", which is often used against homosexuals. Anyone with an education in English grammar knows that effeminate does NOT mean "homosexual" - and neither does its biblical Greek word, "malakos." The Strong's Concordance defines this word as "soft, i.e. fine (clothing), effeminate." The Webster's New World Dictionary of 1951 defines it as "having the qualities generally attributed to women, as weakness, gentleness, delicacy, etc. Unmanly, weak, soft, decadent." Pro-Baseball player Billy Bean, for example, is homosexual but is not effeminate. Cunningham further states, "On the other hand, Michael Jackson was a heterosexual who was highly effeminate.* **I know about as many heterosexuals as homosexuals who behave in this manner.** *In fact, only a small minority of homosexuals are effeminate. The main reason that most homosexuals have been able to hide in the "closet" so well is because* they are NOT effeminate. Being effeminate is not a homosexual trait; it is an "unmasculine" trait.

However, the context of the word as it is used in Scripture indicates nothing in relation to mannerisms. The Bible itself defines this word. Jesus used this very same word when He compared John the Baptist's clothing to that worn in king's houses:

" But what went ye out for to see? A man clothed in soft [malakos] raiment. Behold, they that wear soft [malakos] raiment are in kings' houses." (Matthew 11:8).

Those that live in king's houses dress effeminate (malakoi), while John's clothing was merely a rough camel's skin. The daintiness and niceties of a royal court, where every luxury is indulged, is a perfect example of the biblical use of "effeminate." It harkens back to Deuteronomy 22:5, "Neither shall a man put on a woman's garment: for all that do so are abomination unto the LORD thy God" – an effeminate behavior that has been rampant among many heterosexual men for thousands of years. I am reminded of an episode of the TV show <u>THE GOLDEN GIRLS</u> in which the character, Sophia, discusses her heterosexual son with her daughter Dorothy and roommate Blanche:

SOPHIA: Dorothy, I never understood why your brother liked to wear women's clothes. Unless he was queer.

BLANCHE: Sophia, people don't say queer anymore, they say gay.

SOPHIA: They say gay if a guy can sing the entire score of "Gigi." But, a six foot three, two hundred pound married man with kids who likes to dress up like Dorothy Lamour, I think you have to go with queer!"

To use these verses solely against homosexuals is totally in error, and a convoluted attempt to push anti-gay propaganda. The sad thing is that, by attributing these verses to homosexuality, those to whom it is really meant happily continue on in their ways, content that the Lord has nothing to chastise them for. We may not have control over whom and what we are on a basic human level, but we do have control over how we behave and who we love (God commands us to love fully in the total contexts of the three types of loves (Agape, Philo, Eros); and the Lord expects us to behave in a manner which edifies HIM. He must increase and we must decrease, as John the Baptist put it.

We should be proud of who God made us to be, because He created us for His glory, to be His temple. Whether you are gay or straight, if you were created as a female, thank the Lord for creating you as a female and honor Him in your female body. If you were created as a male, thank the Lord for creating you as a male and honor Him in your male body. If God made you as a woman it was because He WANTED a woman, and if He created you as a man it was because He WANTED a man. It's up to you to decide whether you want to live for Christ or live for yourself. To live for Christ is to behave in a manner that properly edifies what HE wants. If you are a man or woman and do not know how to "fit" into your male or female body, simply ask the Lord to help you; and to the church I say that such men and women are in need the gentle strength and support of your compassion and understanding and mercy, rather than a wagging and bitter tongue of hate and condemnation and self-righteousness. Don't confuse being gay with being unmanly, nor being lesbian *with being unwomanly. There is no law against being gay or lesbian, but God is clear that He expects us to align ourselves with the physical body He has blessed us with. We were bought with the price of God's blood; we are not our own property. And a believer's body is specifically the Temple of God. Let God not find confusion in His temple, for it is not HE that is the author of confusion.*

Unfortunately, because these verses have been re-interpreted in modern times to refer to homosexuals, the so-called ex-gay ministries, in their aforementioned ceaseless cause to make Stepford Husbands of homosexual men and women and even children, have tried to use Paul's phrase, "and such were some of you" as evidence that homosexuals can "change" to heterosexuality, and many homosexuals have been deceived by this lie, and have been severally psychologically harmed by it; and others have inflicted physical mutilations on themselves or have committed suicide.

But Paul was speaking to sexually debauched and effeminate men as just the same among a long list of offenders - especially to those wealthy and educated heterosexual men in Greece and Rome who participated in the very common practice of taking young teenagers into their home to educate them and engage in sexual activity with them (the parents of the children and the wives of the teachers knew full well AND APPROVED of what was involved, and it was considered a great honor for a child to be taken in by the Teachers for these practices - the sexual acts were part of the package). If you saw the movie 300, which is a very loose retelling of the army of the ancient Spartans, who were well known for their adult-with-adult-only bisexual fornication, you'll have noted the Spartan king's disgusted reference to "those boy-lovers in Athens". These deeds by the Greeks were well known. And, the near worshipful adoration of the male body in Greek society was so prevalent that women were even forbidden to attend the ancient Olympic Games because the athletes were required to go naked in order to sport and flaunt their bodies. Such wickedness should be enough to cause any godly man or woman - straight or gay - to want to vomit.

So these activities, condemned by Paul, are not historical secrets, but are known through the world over - and Paul rightly rebuked them, as we do also. Perhaps our Christian society should stop misplacing biblical references like this by wrongfully accusing homosexuals, and start to place biblical criticisms where they rightly belong. If the Christian community desires to launch a public tirade against societal immorality, perhaps directing it towards the rampant heterosexual adultery and divorce and the total inundation of sex and violence in the entertainment industry might be a better and more productive place to start - rather than railing against a group of people just because they aren't attracted to certain genitals.

But I myself recommend that Christians do exactly what Jesus Himself commanded, which is that we ought not to raise up our voices in the streets like riotous fools, with protesting and picketing, entangling religion with politics; but rather, remember that Christ said MY KINGDOM IS <u>NOT</u> OF THIS WORLD, and therefore we must STOP trying to create God's Kingdom here on this earth with this absurd attempt to enforce the Gospel on the People by force of Law (instead of by the individual's willful acceptance by faith); and when any society refuses to hear God's Word, we MUST NOT retaliate by forcing our religion upon them by law, but instead simply wipe their dust off our feet and MOVE ON. Let GOD be judge, and leave the Right of Vengeance in GOD'S hands as He Himself commanded. Those who dare to usurp from God His sole

Right of Vengeance will face this punishment: "that measure which you mete will be measured to you and you will be judged with the judgment that you judge others." We have the right to determine right from wrong and to live righteously - but we do not have the power to judge individuals with condemnation; and we most certainly do not have the authority to use God's holy and precious Scriptures as a weapon against mankind ("for the weapons of our warfare are NOT CARNAL... for we wrestle NOT against flesh and blood!").

LOVE our neighbors, DO GOOD to our enemies, and TEACH the Gospel of Christ TO THOSE WHO WILL HEAR: and that is what we've been authorized to do. Be wary of any "Christian" who does contrary to this."

As a Christian and preacher, I do agree that God is the ultimate judge. He will judge the hearts and minds of every human, either "right or wrong". God said in a noble parable (Matthew 13:24-30) "Another parable he put forth unto them, saying, The kingdom of heaven is likened unto a man which sowed good seed in his field: But while men slept, his enemy came and sowed tares among the wheat, and went his way. But when the blade was sprung up, and brought forth fruit, then appeared the tares also. So the servants of the householder came and said unto him, Sir, didst not thou sow good seed in thy field? From whence then hath it tares? He said unto them, an enemy hath done this. The servants said unto him, Wilt thou then that we go and gather them up? But he said, nay; lest while ye gather up the tares, ye root up also the wheat with them. **Let both grow together until the harvest: and in the time of harvest I will say to the reapers, Gather ye** together first the tares, and bind them in bundles to burn them: but gather the wheat into my barn."

I do go on record to say, that it is God that will do the separating of the right from the wrong. I have learned to take my mouth off people as in talking about their character. You never know who is going to be in heaven on that great day. Will it be you, my preach brother, or will it be those who may not look, sing, talk, and dress like us?

God gives every human a measure of faith to believe and as John 3:16 (Amp.) states, *"For God so greatly loved and dearly prized the world that He [even] gave up His only (unique) Son, so that whoever believes in (trusts in, clings to, relies on) Him shall not perish (come to destruction, be lost) but have eternal (everlasting) life."* So, excuse me pastor, start loving, and stop judging ---for it is God that has the final say who is saved or not! The question is... "Will you be there on that Great Gett'n up morning?"

Chapter 19

Excuse Me Pastor, Don't Violate Me!

It was Sunday morning and the Spirit of God was moving throughout the entire church. Pastor preached so hard that he had to take his tie and robe off and many came to Christ as he extended to everyone the invitation of discipleship. I was seated on the front row with the other ministers and could feel the power of God moving. People were on their feet worshipping and praising God for the Word that had just gone forth. I can remember how good I felt as I witnessed God move through my pastor.

As soon as he finished, he gave another invitation for people to come for prayer as well. People were getting out of their seats, running to the altar, and pastor called one of the senior ministers up to pray for the people and for those who had given their lives to Christ. Pastor immediately left the pulpit area and he beckoned me to follow him. I thought that it was mighty strange that he would call me to follow him since he was going back to change his clothes to prepare to come back out to greet the people. Then he asked me to lock the door. He said, "Did you enjoy service today," and I said, "Yes sir." He started pulling his clothes off as he was talking and he started to approach me as he got down to his pants and I could not even look at him. He began to ask me questions about the Single's Ministry and how it was going. I started to feel a little awkward. He came closer and I said, "I sent you an email of everything that was going on with the single's ministry." He then remembered he got the email but never read it.

He then went back to the front and proceeded to pull his pants down and I started praying, "Lord, this man is trying to come on to me sexually and trying to violate me." I think I was 30 plus years of age and he was a muscular type of guy. This was weird for him to ask me questions as he finished preaching a spirit-filled message. I prayed that God would allow someone to knock on the door, since this man had gotten down to pulling his underwear off and the Spirit of God was telling me he was trying to violate me. He looked at me in a desperate way, standing nude, as if I was supposed to come and do something to him. Suddenly God allowed a knock at the door. He rushed to put his clothes back on and it was the church treasurer. I hurried out of there like I was a fictional character.

I stayed at that church six months prior to this event and never told anyone until writing this portion of the book. I knew what pastor was up too. I left that Sunday and never came back. I felt violated and if he had tried to make me do something sexual, I would have not been in a spiritual frame of mind. I would have taken one of the chairs and thrown it at him and fought him physically that day. It would have been my word against his.

I did not want my pastor to come on to me. I felt violated in the worst way. I got into my car and tears rolled down my face. I started to pray out loud that God would comfort me. This Sunday was a blessed day, but yet a day from "Hell." Who wants to be violated anyway? Especially by the man of

God that is supposed to watch and give an accounting of your soul. I later heard that he divorced his wife due to infidelity with other men.

I received a call some years later from the ex-wife and she asked me if he tried to come on to me and I never gave her an answer. I stated, "That is something you need to deal with in your own mind." It was not my place to open her wounds deeper. The only thing she said to me was that he had several younger guys' phone numbers in his phone and on the phone bill…my number was not one of them, but she wanted to see why I left the church so quickly that Sunday. This was all a tragedy played out through Satan's plan to destroy my life, as well as other. I would not give him power to do that type of despicable act to me. However, the pastor allowed Satan to use him and it destroyed him, his family, and his ministry.

As the above Scripture reference points out, "Satan comes to steal, and to kill, and to destroy, but Christ came to give us life more abundantly (John 10:10)."

For so long, we in the church have swept this under the carpet and the victims may later turn out to be ones who victimize others. Pastors or preachers are at the forefront of the limelight. All stories that are told may not be true; however, all the stories are not lies from the members of that local body. It happens all too often but we as members only say, "The pastor has flesh like any other man." This is stinking-thinking! Think about your little girls and boys who go to church with the expectation of learning the Word of God and in turn come back home scared, battered and torn because some pastor counted them to be less comely to that local body. Yes, the pastor has a flesh, but I do not think that all members go to church to be victimized by the one who is beholden to them and has shared the precious Word of God.

Moreover, the sexually abused person often denies the abuse, mislabels it, or at least minimizes the damage. The enemy goes unrecognized or misunderstood, so the victim cannot fight the battle. Once the war is avoided, then something must be done with the wounded heart that cries out for solace and hope. The cry must be either heard or squelched. Sadly, the choice is usually to stifle the groan. What normally mutes the cry is the internal dynamic that promotes denial, mislabeling, or minimization. The dynamic involves the subtle workings of shame and contempt that serve to keep the soul frozen and the warmth of life at a distance.

Many of you might question the essence of this writing, but there is both deeper and less hidden meaning behind what I am conveying. People do not want to take part of any entity if someone tries to or does steal the breath of life from them willfully. Some would rather sit at home and listen to a biblical message from the televangelist and never truly enjoy what it means to be part of a united, august body of believers that actually cares about their well-being.

Moreover, the victimizer always lurks or preys on victims that are timid, shy, and not skilled in the Word. Nevertheless, some are skilled, but they have fallen prey to the assailant's tactics to be part of the in crowd. People are looking up to their leaders to be loved and not to add stress or drama to their lives. Just as my situation mentioned in the beginning, I only wanted solid spiritual leadership in my life, but the end result was that of being violated by some pastor who had childhood problems that were never managed.

My heart goes out to those who are struggling to find what I was looking for as well. I have heard stories from others that are too numerous to mention but I do believe them. I see tears that are shed but no one knows why they are crying. I have heard of testimonies from those individuals who have actually experienced trauma from so called "loving pastors" but their only ploy was to violate. I cry out for those individuals who only have a whisper of voice to deal with traumatic experiences similar to mine.

Chapter 20

Excuse Me Pastor, Can You Pray for Me?

"For the LORD will not abandon His people on account of His great name, because the LORD has been pleased to make you a people for Himself. Moreover, as for me, far be it from me that I should sin against the LORD by ceasing to pray for you; but I will instruct you in the good and right way. Only fear the LORD and serve Him in truth with all your heart; for consider what great things He has done for you" (I Samuel12: 22-24).

"And they came to a place which was named Gethsemane: and he saith to his disciples, Sit ye here, while I shall pray. And he taketh with him Peter and James and John, and began to be sore amazed and to be very heavy; And saith unto them, My soul is exceeding sorrowful unto death: tarry ye here, and watch. And he went forward a little, and fell on the ground, and prayed that, if it were possible, the hour might pass from him. And he said, Abba, Father, all things are possible unto thee; take away this cup from me: nevertheless not what I will, but what thou wilt. And he cometh, and findeth them sleeping, and saith unto Peter, Simon, sleepest thou? Couldest not thou watch one hour? Watch ye and pray, lest ye enter into temptation. The spirit truly is ready, but the flesh is weak" (Mark 14:32-38).

Now, I know there were no pastors (by titles) in the Old Testament but the prophets who would intercede on behalf of the people. But Samuel being the prophet and Jesus our prophet, priest and King interceded for us as He still does. This is true today as much as it was way back then. Pastors need to pray for their flock. No matter how tattered, torn and disgruntled we are, it is the duty of pastor to pray for us as Samuel and Jesus did.

I remember being at one of the churches that I attended and we were having a revival. There was an evangelist or pastor and he made the statement that one of his members asked him to pray for them and he said something which hurt my heart, "I will not pray for you because you do not pay your tithes."

What a tragic statement to make before a body of people that did not know him and knowing that he had to give an account for the souls that he shepherded. I went to my pastor at that time and told him that we should not invite him back to the church to minister because it sends a wrong message of what a pastor's role should be. My pastor did not accept my coming to him in that fashion, but it was not right. Just because someone does not pay their tithes in the form of money does not preclude any pastor from praying for his flock. Many of the other members of the church heard him say this and, needless to say, our pastor finally listened to us. It is not the tithe that Jesus is concerned about, it is the soul of the person. Tithing is more than money. It is your time, talent and resources. Who knows whether that lady could have been one of the ones praying for him and using the time God had given her to minister to others.

Sometimes I suspect that some pastors think that they are "little gods" and try to belittle those who are less fortunate than they. It is everyone's duty to pray for each other. If my pastor did not pray for me, I knew how to pray for myself and that is why Jesus' crucifixion caused the veil of the temple to be torn from the top to the bottom, opening the door for whosoever to come before him to get their needs met during prayer. It is a horrific view for a pastor to say, "I am not going to pray for you," and what gives them that right when Jesus in his high priestly prayer in John Chapter 17 (which is really the Lord's Prayer) prayed for us that we would be one.

Saints, stop getting in all of the prayer lines and asking them to lay hands on you for prayer; learn how to pray and lay hands on yourselves, because God has given to you the same power through the Holy Spirit. It took me a long time to understand this and I am so glad that Jesus is still interceding on my behalf right now (even when I sin). When my earthly pastor cannot be found, I know that Jesus is always there without any hesitation to pray for me.

There was something about Jesus' prayer life that touched the disciples and showed them they did not know how to pray. They observed him at work engaged in the business of prayer and asked for help. Hear Luke 11:1-4 (ESV) as he records this: *"Now Jesus was praying in a certain place, and when he finished, one of his disciples said to him, "Lord, teach us to pray, as John taught his disciples. "And he said to them, "When you pray, say: "Father, hallowed be your name. Your kingdom come. Give us each day our daily bread, and forgive us our sins, for we ourselves forgive everyone who is indebted to us. And lead us not into temptation..."* Obviously, there was something visible or tangible the disciples saw about his prayer life that made them request a lesson on prayer.

Pastors should often teach prayer by praying in the presence of their disciples. Jesus was not ashamed of modeling prayer. I am convinced that a greater reason for the prayerlessness in the pews emanates from prayerlessness in the pulpit. Pastors need to pray and pray in the presence of their flock. It is amazing that generally pastors do not attend prayer meetings. When I quizzed one pastor about this, I was shocked because he said that his flock felt intimidated by his prayer life. The flock is inspired and taught prayer by observing your prayer life. Jesus was not afraid of intimidating his disciples by His prayer. In our own church movement we have noticed that the All Night prayer meetings and prayer meetings of churches where the local pastors attend the meetings to pray through with the flock, are generally more effective in mobilizing the church members to pray. By the way, when pastors attend prayer meetings, they should do so to pray and not necessarily to lead the meeting. Pastors should take time to enjoy prayer when they are not leading but praying together with others. *When pastors do not attend prayer meetings with the flock they send a message that prayer is not important.* However, Jesus took the opportunity to teach prayer by praying with and before his disciples.

I read an excerpt from the Prayer Meeting First Aid Kit by Keeney Dickenson and it really speaks to the heart of this portion the book. He states, "Every pastor should without exception be a man of prayer. Empty messages flow from empty men. How can God speak through us if we have not allowed Him to speak to us? The church will never be a 'House of Prayer' until the pastor is a 'man of prayer.'"

Many churches seem to be completely disoriented to God. They have come to rely on the tradition of the past or the innovation of the present. It appears that the people of God have become strangers to the ways of God. The tragic words of Judges 2:10 seem to describe the condition of the church today, "When all that generation had been gathered to their fathers, another generation arose after them who did not know the Lord nor walk the way his father had done for Israel."

The church is no longer intimately anchored to the Father in the prayer closet and Scripture. The pastors of today cannot honestly say with the apostles, "We will give ourselves continually to prayer and the ministry of the Word" (Acts 6:4).

Therefore, we preach sermons from our bookshelves rather than our prayer closets; messages that are pathetic rather than prophetic. The prayerlessness in the pulpit has perpetuated the worldliness in the pew. *Prayerless pews are the offspring of prayerless pulpits.* Oh, that pastors would recover the spirit of Samuel as he proclaimed to the people, "Moreover, as for me, far be it from me that I should sin against the Lord in ceasing to pray for you; but I will teach you the good and right way" (1 Samuel 12:23).

When the White House holds a press conference, people representing the president of the United States stand behind a podium and speak on his behalf. The podium bears the seal of the White House and carries with it the authority of the president himself. We assume that those who represent the president in this setting have spent hours seated with the president, becoming well acquainted with his views on certain subjects. Therefore, when behind the podium they only speak that which they have heard directly from the president.

Every Sunday, pastors step behind the pulpit to speak a word on behalf of God. Many of those pulpits bear a cross that carries with it an image of power and authority. The people in the pews assume that the one in the pulpit has spent hours in the presence of God, becoming well acquainted with His heart and mind concerning the subject of the sermon. However, in many cases these assumptions are false because of chronic prayerlessness in the life of the preacher.

The church is desperate for praying pastors. One of our most subtle temptations is to rely on insight and innovation, rather than intercession. The words of Isaiah are an indictment against the church in our day: "Woe to those who go down to Egypt for help, and rely on horses, who trust in chariots because they are very strong, but do not look to the Holy One of Israel, nor seek the Lord" (Isaiah 31:1). Our ministries are shaped more by trends in society than the travail of the soul. The travesties of the modern church are pulpits that are plagued and contaminated with prayerlessness.

It is imperative that the church return to her God-given identity as the house of prayer. Houses of prayer are nurtured and developed by men of prayer, men whose hearts turn to the Lord early, daily, and continually in a spirit of prayer. Pastors must be trailblazers back to the prayer closet. The power of God rests upon men who have a mind that is bathed in prayer, and a ministry that is based on prayer. Could it be that our prayer meetings are lifeless because our prayer closets are empty?

The reality is that the depth of our ministry of the Word will never exceed the depth of our ministry of prayer. The two are inseparable. In pastoral ministry, prayer without the ministry of the Word is fruitless, and the ministry of the Word without prayer is rootless. Oh, that God would raise up pastors whose praying surpasses their preaching!" This is my sincere prayer and confession as well.

Chapter 21

Excuse Me Pastor, Don't Hinder My Praise!

"And when he heard that it was Jesus of Nazareth, he began to cry out, and say, Jesus, thou Son of David, have mercy on me. And many charged him that he should hold his peace: but he cried the more a great deal, Thou Son of David, have mercy on me. And Jesus stood still, and commanded him to be called. And they call the blind man, saying unto him, Be of good comfort, rise; he calleth thee. And he, casting away his garment, rose, and came to Jesus. And Jesus answered and said unto him, What wilt thou that I should do unto thee? The blind man said unto him, Lord, that I might receive my sight. And Jesus said unto him, Go thy way; thy faith hath made thee whole. And immediately he received his sight, and followed Jesus in the way" (Mark 10:46-52).

I was at church one Sunday and there was a spirit that nagged me. I stood up and shouted "Amen" loudly to what the speaker was saying; the Spirit of God was moving in the church service. I felt someone pulling my jacket and, to my surprise, it was one of the pastors. I was told by the pastor to "sit down." It bothered my spirit even as others started to give their shouts of "Amen" simultaneously. Other people saw what the pastor had done to me but they did not say anything to him at the time. I sat and my spirit was broken as the senior pastor was about to give the message shortly after this fiasco. I started to leave church after that situation and other ministers stopped me from leaving because they saw the expression on my face. I began to take my paper out and started writing to include what happened in this portion of the book. There were others who saw and felt the same way I did but were uncomfortable saying anything to this particular pastor. So, I started writing to express my feelings instead of getting in verbal conflict. I was going to talk to the pastor later after I had calmed down so that I could address him in a proper manner.

As I began to pen, "Some people do not know what you have gone through just to make it to church or any worship service for that matter. Some do not clap, shout or lift holy hands; some think that you are disturbing the worship service because they do not know the story behind your praise. I felt like Pastor Shirley Caesar's "Shouting John" when he stated, "God gave me all this land and you do not want me dance or shout in your church, so I will shout right here."

God has a way of showing the true proclivity of others who think they know what you have been through. It is interesting that, at the same time, this pastor was preaching on praise every Wednesday night. Their insensitive thoughts to the Spirit of God were maligned with the thoughts of the devil, knowing well what was spoken to me. The devil always wants to "Steal, kill and destroy" (John 10: 10). Some people will flip the script on you when they do not know what you are praising God for as well. I knew this pastor's thoughts were of a hypocritical spirit in which they allowed the enemy to use them to try to break my spirit from praising God. People and pastors have to realize that you do not know why God has people to shout out loud in the praise and worship service. I sincerely know that praising God out loud can change the atmosphere and I noticed that others wanted to break forth in praise to God as well because we could sense His presence. I do not know what they were praising God for, but I know I had a testimony behind my praise and God understood my sincere desires.

I listened to the pastor and it did bother my spirit, so I sat down. I had to pray and praise in a different way to get myself out of the carnal state. The pastor and I would not have been proud if I responded negatively. I could not really hear what the senior pastor was preaching about because my mind was so consumed with words that would be unlawful for me to utter in a worship service. However, it was just a set up so that God could use the senior pastor to preach a heavenly sermon that would bless the people of God. Sometimes, we think the struggle is against us, but it is really against God and His Word that is about to go forth. I also came to the conclusion that some pastors, or anyone for that matter, think they have killed your will but they are only being used to push a person closer to the presence of God. When the devil pushes you to the point of testing by his speech and the elements of his will, God always sends a divine Word to counteract those elements and will lift your spirit to new dimensions in Christ.

As the main reference, Scripture calls him "the blind man" or in the synoptic gospels records him as "Blind Bartimaeus." He was told to stop crying out and bothering Jesus because He basically was not concerned about him. But the more they tried to stop him, he cried more and more to attract the attention of Jesus. The disciples did not understand that God was using Bartimaeus' praise as the preeminence of why Jesus came through Jericho to show forth God's command and get others to follow Him. They also did not understand that his cry catapulted or was used as a "stepping stone" to show that Jesus can heal any sickness and or disease.

However, Jesus heard him and said, "Bring him to me," and asked the question (Author's Interpretation), "What do you want me to do for you?" Bartimaeus responded, "I want to see again." His cry was a cry of faith although one of his five senses was not in operation, there was a sixth sense operating within him called *"faith"* that ultimately got him to this point.

That is the question that God is articulating to us, "What do you want me to do for you? As I looked at my broken spirit during the worship service Jesus was asking me, "What do you want me to do for you, even though your praise was stifled?" He is asking the same question to those of us who cry, the lips that do not speak, the hearts that are broken, the poor in spirit, and the lame that wants to walk, "What do you want me to do for you?"

All we have to do is to keep crying, keep shouting, and keep pressing toward the one that heals and not the pastors that try to derail our healing. It is in those times that praise has to go forth. No one can understand your cry. No one can see the tears that are never shed but Jesus! We have to be bold in faith to deal with those Pharisees who do not understand our story.

After church was over, the pastor came back to me and the enemy was trying to use him again by saying, "You are a showman." I said, "Listen, you do not know my story. You do not know why I praise and how God brought me out and is still bringing me out of things. So please do not judge my praise." Someone quickly pulled him away from me and the pastor never really apologized to me that day but said "I will not sit by you again." I do believe the pastor's actions served as a catalyst to set off a domino effect to spread what God was about to do with saints and the non-believers that were in attendance in the worship service. I later talked with the senior pastor and explained what happened and I received a phone call from the pastor that made the statement to me. He quickly apologized! I did accept his apology because I do not believe in being a man of God and not having a forgiving spirit about me. The pastor stated they were joking with me and I felt in the joking, you have to understand a person's personality when the Spirit of God is moving. It is not that I do like to have fun in the Spirit of God, but there is a time and place for all things and I think the timing was off and they were not in a mode to understand where I was at that time with my praise to God.

I cannot help but place some lyrics to a Gospel Song by Pastor John P. Kee, **Life and Favor:** that says the following (feat. James Fortune, Isaac Carree & Lejuene Thompson):

Some people have seen where God has brought you from
They really don't understand it
They don't know your story.

You don't know my story
You don't know the things that I've come through

You cannot imagine
The pain the trials I've had to endure

You don't know my story
You don't know the day He set me free
You cannot imagine
The strongholds and the walls that severed me

In all God has been faithful to me
He promised He would never leave me
My story proves that God can use me
Deliverance is my testimony
You don't know -- my story!
You don't know -- my story.

You don't know my story
The anguish and the guilt that consume me
Grateful I can tell it
For no more shall the shackles condemn me

You don't know my story
For if you did you would lift up your hands

So just let me tell you
By faith you may as well brdeak out and dance.

In all God has been faithful to me
He promised He would never leave me
My story proves that God can use me
Deliverance is my testimony

You don't know -- my story!
You don't know -- my story.

Through my testimony that the blood of the lamb
delivered again
Now I have a testimony;
Favor's upon me

Grace and Mercy, Love and Peace Abound
All in you I've found
A lord that will not never leave me
(He won't forsake me.)

You don't know my story

I'm delivered, here's my story
Life and Favor upon me He brought me out
You don't know it, let me tell it
Life and favor upon me He brought me out

God of Mercy He who loves me
Life and favor upon me He brought me out
Oh how wondrous is my story
Life and favor He brought me out
Can't imagine what I've gone through
Life and favor upon me He brought me out
Can't imagine what I've gone through
Can't imagine.

I'm delivered, here's my story
Life and favor upon me He brought me out
You don't know it, let me tell it
Life and favor upon me He brought me out

God of mercy He who loves me
Life and favor upon me He brought me out
Oh how wondrous is my story

Life and favor upon me He brought me out

Can't imagine what I've gone through
Life and favor upon me He brought me out
I'm delivered, here's my story
Life and favor upon me He brought me out

Can't imagine what I've gone through
Life and favor upon me He brought me out
God of mercy, He who loves me
Life and favor upon me He brought me out

Oh how wondrous is my story
Life and favor upon me He brought me out
Can't imagine what I've gone through
Life and favor upon me He brought me out

I also read an article (Author Unknown) that encouraged me through this period of my life. "When the Israelites returned to Judah after being taken captive for several years during the time of the Prophet Nehemiah, they discovered that the walls of the city had been destroyed by the enemies. A message was sent to Nehemiah who was serving under King Artaxerxes about the state of things in Jerusalem.

Nehemiah prayed and fasted that the king would grant his request to go down to Jerusalem to build the walls, the king granted his request and he went and started the work. As he commenced the work, some people came to discourage. They mocked him, particularly Sanballat and Gesham (They were enemies of God). There are many Sanballats and Geshams in our world today. They will come in different forms to discourage you when you are making progress in your career, your business and projects.

Many people do not want you to succeed in your God-given dreams and will try every avenue to stop you. Particularly if you are trusting God for your breakthrough in every area of your life. In Nehemiah Chapter 6, Nehemiah continued the building of the walls of Judah in spite of the discouragement and mockery by his enemies particularly Sanballat, Tobiah, and Gesham the Arab. They sent some letters to him to discourage him from building.

Nehemiah 6:2-3, "So Sanballat and Gesham sent a message asking me to meet them at one of the villages in the plain of Ono. But I realized they were plotting to harm me, so I replied by sending this message to them, "I am engaged in a great work, so I can't come. Why should I stop working to come and meet with you?"

When you are working on a life changing project, dream, destiny changing business, enemies will try to distract you. They will say many discouraging things to stop you, and they will even mock you. They will want the project to fail, so they can laugh at you, but you have to remain steadfast to your dreams. You must be determined to achieve your heart's desire.

Nehemiah said, "Four times they sent the same message and each time I gave the same reply" (Nehemiah 6:4). We have to learn to be consistent in our goals. Never sway from what God has mandated you to do even if it has to cost you something in the process.

In chapter 6:9, Nehemiah said, "They were just trying to intimidate us, imagining that they could discourage us and stop the work. So I continued the work with even greater determination."

When all that didn't work, they tried using a close person to Nehemiah to work against him; they used Shemaiah the son of Delaiah to frighten him. He told him a lie by saying, "Let us meet together inside the temple of God and bolt the doors shut. Your enemies are coming to kill you tonight." But I replied, "Should someone in my position run from danger?" I realized God had not spoken to him, but he had uttered this prophecy against me because Tobiah and Sanballat had hired him. They were hoping to intimidate me and make me sin. Then they would be able to accuse and discredit me (Nehemiah 6:10-13). "

You see, when you are making progress in your destiny, in your business, in your career, ministry, family life, marriage; people will try all sorts of things to discourage you. Please do not listen to them, and follow your heart. Especially if you are being guided by God, you will know how to respond, and you will surely be successful. Be determined to succeed regardless of whatever obstacles that may come your way.

Even in ministry work, people will try to discourage you so that you don't succeed. Always allow the words of God to be your guide in everything that you do.

Chapter 22

Excuse Me Pastor, Do You Really Love Me?

"Now the tax collectors and [notorious and especially wicked] sinners were all coming near to [Jesus] to listen to Him. And the Pharisees and the scribes kept muttering and indignantly complaining, saying, This man accepts and receives and welcomes [¹preeminently wicked] sinners and eats with them. So He told them this parable: What man of you, if he has a hundred sheep and should lose one of them, does not leave the ninety-nine in the wilderness (desert) and go after the one that is lost until he finds it? And when he has found it, he lays it on his [own] shoulders, rejoicing. And when he gets home, he summons together [his] friends and [his] neighbors, saying to them, rejoice with me, because I have found my sheep which was lost. Thus, I tell you, there will be more joy in heaven over one [especially] wicked person who repents (changes his mind, abhorring his errors and misdeeds, and determines to enter upon a better course of life) than over ninety-nine righteous persons who have no need of repentance" (Luke 15:17 Amp).

I cannot help but talk about my dog, Charlie, in this book. I remember I received a call at work because my dog, Charlie, had almost gotten his paw bitten off by an untrained big pit-bull who belonged to a new neighbor. Anyone who knows or has seen Charlie, he is small Miniature Schnauzer, fifteen pounds soaking wet, but he is the only child that I have in my household and some people do not think of their pets as their children. After all, we have to pay for their food, shots, treats, toys and clean-up behind them when they make a mess around the house. As I continue with the story of Charlie and the untrained big pit-bull, I was so worried because blood was everywhere on him, His paw was dangling, blood was in my car, on my shirt and he would not stop whimpering. As I rushed to take him in to the veterinarian, she stated, "I am glad you got here in time. He would have died." He had to undergo anesthesia and surgery. Mind you, I had no one to keep him so I took some family sick time.

As I returned to work after a week of looking after Charlie, I wrote out my leave form and placed it in my supervisor's box because I do not steal time and I want to do the right thing. My supervisor stated to me in a very boisterous and mean voice, "Michael Shine, This is not going to fly!"

I did not know what she was talking about since she was screaming in the hallway of my professional place of employment. I went into her office and she was still upset. I do not know why she took that tone with me and she said, "Dogs are not family and you need to take some vacation time for this."

My voice amplified and everyone on our floor heard us arguing. I stated to her, "Although I do not have any kids, what would you have done if your son got bitten by a wolf, snake or big untrained dog?"

She stated, "I would have let someone call the ambulance and take him to the doctor and go with him there."

I stated to her, "I do not have that pleasure or luxury with Charlie seeing that he is a dog, family member and needed help due to the state he was in."

She later wrote me up for being insubordinate and I told her I was not going to sign the form because I did not agree with her management style and the tone she took with me as well. I did not cuss her nor did I threaten her. So, she called the City's Chief of Operations down to talk to her and he said, "Let me talk to Michael." He told me, "Just show her a little respect and that is all she wants."

I stated to him, "I do not mean you any disrespect, but respect must be earned! She may not look at my dog, Charlie, as a family member nor does the City, but I tend to take care of my family no matter if they are pets and they actually live in my house. I further stated that the write up was not fair as well. I was not trying to beat the system. "She could have easily with a calm voice recited or showed me some documentation regarding what is deemed a family member by our job standards, but she did not. She also talked to me like I was a child and has taken advantage of several undocumented lunches and time off that everyone in our office knew about. It was just not fair."

He took the paper and tore it up, but the unsigned document still remained in my personnel file and that still was not fair. So, I just took the high road and took the vacation time and our relationship has gotten better.

Given the above story, it shows the love and compassion that a pastor should have for his sheep or anyone for that matter.

Although Charlie is a dog, everyone still needs love. There is a line in the movie *The Color Purple* that says, "It pisses God off when you walk by the color purple and don't notice it." In other words, everyone needs love.

The above line from the movie is rich and packed with meaning. This is the same way pastors should look at people that visit the local church that they pastor. One of Jesus' favorite metaphors for spiritual leadership, one He often used to describe Himself, was that of a shepherd--a person who tends God's flock. A shepherd leads, feeds, nurtures, comforts, corrects, and protects--responsibilities that belong to every church leader. In fact, the word pastor means shepherd. Peter wrote these words to elders who would have been familiar with sheep and shepherding:

I exhort the elders among you ... shepherd the flock of God neither ... exercising oversight not under compulsion, but voluntarily, according to the will of God; and not for sordid gain, but with eagerness; nor yet as lording it over those allotted to your charge, but proving to be examples to the flock. And when the Chief Shepherd appears, you will receive the unfading crown of glory (). "

To give you a more complete picture of your pastor's role, here's a look at the nature of sheep, the task of shepherds, and how they compare to the pastor's role among the church. Note the principles of church leadership it contains--they determine what should fill your pastor's schedule.

Shepherds Are Rescuers

A sheep can be totally lost within a few miles of its home. With no sense of direction and no instinct for finding the fold, a lost sheep usually will walk around in a state of confusion, unrest, and even panic. It needs a shepherd to bring it home.

And so, when Jesus saw the crowds, lost, spiritually disoriented, and confused, He likened them to sheep without a shepherd (). The prophet Isaiah described lost people as those who, like sheep, have gone astray--each one turning to his own way ().

Like lost sheep, lost people need a rescuer--a shepherd--to lead them to the safety of the fold. A pastor does that by pointing the lost toward Jesus, the Good Shepherd who lays down His life for the sheep ().

Shepherds Are Feeders

Sheep spend most of their lives eating and drinking, but they are indiscriminate about their diet. They don't know the difference between poisonous and non-poisonous plants. Therefore the shepherd must carefully guard their diet and provide them with pasture rich with nutrients. In His encounter with him described in John 21, Jesus drove home to Peter the importance of feeding the sheep. Twice in His command to Peter, Jesus used the Greek term *bosko*, which means "I feed" (vs. 15, 17).

The pastor's goal is not to please the sheep, but to feed them--not to tickle their ears, but to nourish their souls. He is not to offer merely light snacks of spiritual milk, but the substantial meat of biblical truth. Those who fail to feed the flock are unfit to be shepherds (;).

Shepherds Are Leaders

Peter challenged his fellow elders to "shepherd the flock of God among you" by "exercising oversight" (). God entrusted them with the authority and responsibility of leading the flock. Pastors are accountable for how they lead, and the flock for how they follow ().

Besides teaching, the pastor exercises oversight of the flock by the example of his life. Being a pastor requires getting in among the sheep. It is not leadership from above so much as leadership from within. An effective pastor does not herd his sheep from the rear but leads them from the front. They see him and imitate his actions.

The most important asset of spiritual leadership is the power of an exemplary life. instructs a church leader to, "Pay close attention to yourself and to your teaching; persevere in these things, for as you do this you will ensure salvation both for yourself and for those who hear you."

Shepherds Are Protectors

Sheep are almost entirely defenseless--they can't kick, scratch, bite, jump, or run. When attacked by a predator, they huddle together rather than running away. That makes them easy prey. Sheep need a protective shepherd in order to survive.

Christians need similar protection from error and those who spread it. Pastors guard their spiritual sheep from going astray and defend them against the savage wolves that would ravage them. Paul admonished the pastors at Ephesus to stay alert and to protect the churches under their care:

Be on guard for yourselves and for all the flock, among which the Holy Spirit has made you overseers, to shepherd the church of God which He purchased with His own blood. I know that after my departure savage wolves will come in among you, not sparing the flock; and from among your own selves men will arise, speaking perverse things, to draw away the disciples after them ().

Shepherds Are Comforters

Sheep lack a self-preservation instinct. They are so humble and meek that if you mistreat them, they are easily crushed in spirit and can simply give up and die. The shepherd must know his sheep's individual temperaments and take care not to inflict excessive stress. Accordingly, a faithful pastor adjusts his counsel to fit the need of the person to whom he ministers. He must "admonish the unruly, encourage the fainthearted, help the weak, and be patient with all" ().

The Good Shepherd and His Under-Shepherds

Jesus is the perfect example of a loving shepherd. He epitomizes everything that a spiritual leader should be. Peter called Him the "Chief Shepherd" (). He is our great Rescuer, Leader, Guardian, Protector, and Comforter.

Church leaders are under-shepherds who guard the flock under the Chief Shepherd's watchful eye (). Theirs is a full-time responsibility because they minister to people who, like sheep, often are vulnerable, defenseless, undiscerning, and prone to stray.

Shepherding the flock of God is an enormous task, but to faithful pastors it brings the rich reward of the unfading crown of glory, which will be awarded by the Chief Shepherd Himself at His appearing (). If your pastor is faithfully carrying out the duties required in his job title, remember to follow this admonition of Scripture:

"Obey your leaders and submit to them, for they keep watch over your souls as those who will give an account. Let them do this with joy and not with grief, for this would be unprofitable for you" ().

Chapter 23

How to Confront Your Pastor

Readers sometimes write in and ask me if I think it is a good idea for them to have a meeting and confront a controlling pastor regarding his abusive behavior. These readers hope to facilitate a type of "intervention" where they can attempt to show such a man the error of his ways and try to motivate him to repent and change. Although this may sound like a worthy endeavor, there are some very important reasons to *not* do so unless you are properly prepared. Consider the following:

First, regarding the question itself, "Should I confront my pastor?" I want to point out that the terms "my" and "pastor" really do not apply to an authoritarian dictator who passes himself off as an under-shepherd of Christ. Such a man is not operating as a genuine pastor at all and is therefore nobody's actual pastor. This is a great irony since these leaders flood the pulpits of modern churches and multitudes of members consider these men "their" pastors. That said, let us move on. Christians are certainly free to have a meeting with an errant leader, but sadly these churchmen are almost never open to any change whatsoever regarding their leadership methodologies and they are usually pretty clever at twisting the Scriptures to make their challenger feel totally ungodly for even daring to question them.

No Ears to Hear

A controlling dictator by default usually thinks of the congregation, including their staff, as being *beneath him* and as not being "worthy" enough to bring the Scriptures to him, or not of a high enough "rank" spiritually or ecclesiastically to "speak into" their life. He will typically claim that he will only "hear" from other similar "Senior Pastors" and of course those men won't correct him either because they are all from the same era and are cut from the same cloth.

It is also not uncommon for such a leader to operate in massive narcissistic self-importance, incorrectly thinking of himself as a "Moses" who is receiving instruction directly from God and therefore is not to be questioned or disobeyed. So a man like this will almost invariably be closed off to what you have to say.

The False "Touch Not God's Anointed" Doctrine

Not surprisingly, controlling "pastors" often profess that they are "anointed" and that you are not anointed and so they often invoke the popular "touch not God's anointed" false doctrine to try to discourage would-be challengers from questioning their alleged authority. In order to justify this line of thinking, they misinterpret and misapply the totally unrelated Old Testament account of David and Saul, which clearly shows that they think of themselves as *kings* and think of you as a lesser who is trying to do them harm by merely questioning and correcting them. Of course, this is nonsense. David respected Saul and was determined not to harm (touch) him *physically* (see 1Sam 26:11). This has nothing to do with dealing with *doctrinal* error today. This is not some kind of proof that it is wrong to confront and expose the error of a leader. In fact, ironically, David did correct Saul and he did point out his error (v. 18-20).

Also, the Bible says, *"...the anointing which you have received of Him abides in you..." (1John 2:27)* To gain even more insight, let's consider this verse in fuller context: *These things have I written unto you concerning them that seduce you. But the anointing which you have received of him abides in you, and you need not that any man teach you: but as the same anointing teaches you of all things, and is truth, and is no lie, and even as it has taught you, you shall abide in Him. And now, little children, abide in Him; that, when He shall appear, we may have confidence, and not be ashamed before Him at his coming" (1 John 2:26-28).*

We can gain an even larger context of 1John 2:27 by reading a little earlier on in the chapter, where we see that the passage above is written to "fathers," "young men" and "little children" (see verse 12-14), which essentially means to *all* Christians. This is not written as being something exclusive to pastors / elders. These verses show us that <u>all Christians are anointed</u>, not just pastors. So even within their out-of-context view of the account of David and Saul, these leaders should at least *not* be "touching" you either with their mistreatment and abuses. But, of course, it almost never works out that way because, regardless of their claims to the contrary, men like this do not truly recognize and acknowledge the basic *equality* of all believers (where, while we may have differing roles, we are all equally important). This passage also shows us that we do not even need these men to teach us. God is ultimately our teacher who teaches us through His written Word as illuminated by the Holy Spirit.

There May Be a Significant Risk

Probably something even more important to understand than everything said so far is that having a confrontational meeting with an errant church leader can be a *very risky endeavor* because many such "pastors" are often extremely well trained and/or skilled at "corrective measures" or "damage control." They are usually quite adept at turning and re-corralling their income-producing sheep back securely inside their pens. So be forewarned that unless you are very strong in standing your ground regarding *genuine biblical church authority*, such a man could easily spin you around and turn you toward incorrectly thinking that *you* are being rebellious and that *you* are the one who is in the wrong for daring to question him and not blindly submitting to whatever he commands. This is not an uncommon result of such meetings. These men are usually far more skilled at bringing and "defending" their false doctrine than the average Christian is at bringing and defending true doctrine. So it is very common for beaten down and abused Christians, who have finally gotten up enough strength to barely get one foot out the door of a bad church, to then request such a meeting only to be quickly recaptured and shackled once again to their seats.

Controlling pastors are also usually ready for confrontations with full guns loaded. They see questioning and correction as a challenge to their so-called autonomous authority which they are determined to protect. They typically use fear, manipulation, threats, etc. to try to convince you that you are wrong and they are right. They will probably tell you that they have "heard it all before." They will likely marginalize you, minimize your concerns and make you feel like a rebel, like an unfaithful dime-a-dozen type member that they have "dealt with before."

Also, when these men sense that you may be leaving *their* church, they will typically claim that you need their "release" or "permission" before you can do so. Not only is this a lie (the Bible simply does not teach this), not surprisingly, such permission is rarely if ever granted, especially if you are a significant giver financially and/or are someone who volunteers a lot of their time. In that case you would likely be too valuable to them to lose and they would fight all the harder to keep you, not because they love you, of course, but because they need and want the resources that you bring to the table. Don't forget, to them you are not a person; your value is merely as a *human resource* for them to put to work in furthering their own agenda. So while they may easily be able to afford to lose a "non-core" member, they may not be able to afford to lose you if you are a major contributor in one way or another. Therefore, the closer you are to the "inner circle" the harder they will typically fight and the more manipulation they will employ to try to keep you. I have also seen men like this not fight at all to keep non-core, non-income producing, non-volunteering members who question their teachings. They often consider non-conforming members like this to be nothing more than a time-wasting nuisance and so they are happy to grant them permission to leave the Church.

The truth is you don't need anyone's permission to leave the so-called "care" of such a man. And don't fall for the similar "pastor as your covering" lie. The Lord is our *sole* covering (hedge of protection), never a mere mortal man. Oh, the limits that these ungodly men will push to try to make it seem like they have even God-like attributes and qualities!

So unless you have the *goods*, and the goods are a *working understanding* of what the Bible *really* teaches on the subject of authority and control in the local church, then you put yourself at risk of collapsing under the pressure of the trickery of these men and succumbing to their views. Time and time again we see those who try to meet with and correct authoritarian pastors often just end up right back where they started or even worse off. I know very few Christians who have the knowledge of the Scriptures and the discernment required to battle and withstand this kind of well-engineered emotional onslaught.

My Advice

My advice, based on the Scriptures (and my experience) is this: Once you recognize that you are dealing with a control-based leader, don't bother trying to talk with him, just leave. That is a bold statement for me to make. Control is a very intoxicating drug that affects both the controller and those who are being controlled, and so it is almost impossible to help these men or women help their blinded dependents, except possibly from well outside the situation.

Don't make the mistake of thinking of yourself as being on some mercy mission from God, as if you will be the first person on earth who has warned such a man. It is likely that others, perhaps even many others, have gone before you and have tried to talk some sense into him to no avail and probably even to their own detriment. God doesn't send His sheep to the slaughter. God wants us to first be educated (biblically literate), prepared and ready for spiritual battles like this before jumping in, so that we can defend the faith, defend the Scriptures and firmly stand our ground.

In the meantime and regardless of whether or not you are prepared for such a battle, you really need to *get off of the tyrant's turf* and get back to your own home turf where it is far safer for you and where you can diligently study and gain strength without being subverted by a false "church life." It is very easy to get totally sucked back into the subtle nuances of a cult-like system when you try to work from *within* that system. This is one of the main reasons why it is so important to obey God's command to *come out and be separate.*

And what agreement has the temple of God with idols? For you are the temple of the living God; as God has said, I will dwell in them, and walk in them; and I will be their God, and they shall be my people. Wherefore come out from among them, and be separate, says the Lord, and touch not the unclean thing; and I will receive you. And will be a Father unto you, and you shall be my sons and daughters, saith the Lord Almighty" (2Cor 6:16-18).

You might not understand exactly why obeying this passage is so vital now, but if you come out and study, you will likely eventually see how monumentally important it was to GET OUT OF THERE! I also know from experience that taking this critical step is one of the main reasons that I have been freed and able to study unhindered and grow in more and more discernment over these years. You just can't see the big picture and make the right decisions when you are too close to a problem of this magnitude and are blinded and compromised by its many seductions.

The bottom line is that almost without exception, there is simply no fixing a bad church that is being controlled by an unrepentant tyrant, especially when the members not only allow this behavior, but defend and protect this man and his "right" to abuse them. Such a system usually needs to be discarded, not reformed. So until a dictator and the people who support him repent, it pretty much doesn't matter what you say to such a man. He wants to be king and the people want a king. It's a lose-lose situation. There's nothing that can be done short of a miracle from heaven. And since God is not in the business of circumventing people's free will and forcing them to do things that they don't want to do, don't hold your breath expecting any improvement.

Finally, an onlooker only needs to see the dry lifeless bodies of flies in a pile on the ground to know that there is probably a spider somewhere close by. Don't be the next casualty by remaining in the web of a control-based church. Get detached from this sticky mess now while you still can or you just might find yourself trapped in a silk cocoon.

Chapter 24

Nine (9) Lies about the Pastoral Title

I read an article and it speaks to the heart of this section of the message of the book. The author is not known but I decided to include it in this book. It brings about a thorough revelation regarding "Pastoral Titles" in the Church. It states, *"Most churches today are run using the 'Senior Pastor' model, where one man (almost always with a degree from Bible College) does most of the ministering and is looked up to as "the man of God." Few could deny that pastors are truly the ones who are running the church today. Though it could be argued in a number of places that the "big tithers" run the church and have the pastor under their thumb. Such a sick arrangement is just further proof of the damage being done by this "One-Man Pastor" model. It is wide open to abuse.*

Personally, I get on well with a lot of pastors that I meet. But I guess that writing on this topic will cause people to question my motives and some will accuse me of being "rebellious" and having 'problems with authority', etc. But honestly, this is not the case. I simply believe that it is time for us to examine the facts of the matter and acquaint ourselves with what the Bible truly says. After all, only the truth can make us free. Amazingly enough, in the Book of Acts, which is the history of the first thirty years of the early church, the word 'Pastor' is NOT EVEN MENTIONED ONCE. Which is pretty astounding considering how often we use it today. In fact, even in the whole New Testament the word is only used rarely - especially when referring to ministry 'offices'. And when it does appear, it is found near the bottom of a list of ministries in the church: "It was he who gave some to be apostles, some to be prophets, some to be evangelists, and some to be pastors and teachers..." (Eph 4:11, NIV).

There were elders and 'overseers' (these terms are inter-changeable) in the New Testament church. But that is totally different from the position of "one man pastor" that we have today. So how did pastors end up running everything? And what effect does this have on the church?

Well, when you study history it becomes obvious that we mostly got this concept from Rome - not from the Bible. As Beckham said, "Emperor Constantine developed a church structure that has lasted for seventeen centuries... People go to a building (cathedral) on a special day of the week (Sunday) and someone (a priest, or today, a pastor) does something to them (teaching, preaching, absolution or healing) or for them (a ritual or entertainment) for a price (offerings)."

In most cases, what we are seeing today is the continuation of this "Clergy and Laity" system that dominated the church during the Dark Ages. There is very little difference, really. The titles have changed but apart from that it is basically the old Roman Catholic system of professional 'Priests' running everything. We call them 'pastors' but the position is basically the same.

These are people who have gained a degree from Bible College, and now we pay them to be our "ministers." Never mind the fact that we are ALL supposed to be ministers!

What this results in is two different 'classes' in the church. - The "ministering" class and the "churchgoing" class (or 'laity') which is something that God utterly detests. He cannot stand His people being divided up into 'classes' like this. It is the doctrine of the "Nicolaitans" (Rev 2). But is it really that bad? What harm does it really do?

Below are the specific ways that this "one man pastor" model does enormous harm to the church:

(1) It puts one person on a pedestal - above all others. In many churches this veneration of the pastor closely resembles idolatry. His word is law and the entire church revolves around this one man.

(2) This leads directly to PRIDE. The position that we place these men in is terribly dangerous for them and for the whole church. It is very difficult NOT to develop pride when treated in this way. Pride is the most subtle and spiritually fatal of diseases. It wreaks havoc wherever it finds a home.

(3) Control, manipulation and spiritual abuse become common where power is concentrated in the hands of one 'venerated' figure. Power corrupts. Flattery corrupts. Veneration corrupts. And before you know it, people are being terribly damaged and wounded by the control and the "management techniques" being exerted from the top. Then new teachings on "covering" and "submission" are wheeled out, to lend an air of legitimacy to the oppression that is being visited upon people. Everyone is told to 'submit' and not to question. The "one man pastor" system lends itself to this whole scenario like a hand in a glove. It is virtually made for it.

(4) It turns the church into a bunch of "spectators." In other words, everybody sits around and watches while the 'professionals' do most of the work. It is their "job" after all. This is an absolute disaster. For we ALL have gifts and callings and anointing from God.

(5) The position lends itself to "robes and titles" or perhaps expensive 3piece suits! Jesus said to his disciples, "You are not to be called 'Rabbi,' because you have only one Master and you are all brothers. And do not call anyone on earth 'father,' for you have one Father, and he is in heaven. Nor are you to be called 'teacher,' for you have one Teacher, the Christ." (See Matt 23:5-12, NIV). -None of this seems to stop men from taking on "titles" today.

(6) Many pastors by their nature tend to be "play it safe" types. They don't like the boat being rocked and they are often resistant to real change. The fact that today's church is in the hands of pastors, rather than apostles and prophets (as it should be) who are the "risk-takers" of the church, means that it is slow to react and is easily out-maneuvered by the enemy. We desperately need anointed 'risk-takers' and change-oriented leaders today.

(7) Because the position of pastor is usually the "only job going" in the church, it forces many who are actually evangelists or prophets to become pastors, just so they can get to minister. Often they are quite out of place, and many times this leads to disaster when members are mal-assigned.

(8) All of this creates such a load on the shoulders of the man that is appointed senior pastor, that this job has one of the worst BURNOUT rates in the Western world.

(9) At the end of the day, just like church buildings, the best reason for rejecting this model of leadership is that it is simply NOT IN THE BIBLE.

Some people say that having a 'board of elders' who can hire or fire the pastor keeps all of this in check. Not so. It may keep the "control" side of things down, but the mere fact that they feel the need to "appoint a pastor" just shows how hooked into this system they really are. It is centuries old, and all we are doing is perpetuating it. So how did they do things in the New Testament?

Well, the first thing we need to realize is that the apostles were not "professionals." Apart from Paul they had never been to Bible College. (These were run by the Pharisees!) Most of the apostles were simple fishermen and tax-collectors. But they had spent MUCH TIME WITH JESUS. That was their qualification.

And it is clear that pastors were never in charge of the church. It was the APOSTLES who were given that role. But they never "lorded it over" the people. And wherever they went they appointed elders or overseers (plural) to watch over the church in their absence. Unfortunately, some Bible translations use the word "bishop," which gives the impression of a 'hierarchy'. But this was not in the original. As Greek scholar W.E. Vine states: "'Presbuteros', an elder, is another term for the same person as bishop or overseer. (See

Acts 20:17 with verse 28.) So these were just simple "elders" - that's all.

It was only when the church fell into serious decline and then into Romanism that the complicated "hierarchies" began. Before this, it was all very simple. Perhaps one day it will be so again?

This inspires me and should inspire others to think about the place or the priority in which we place pastors. This is not to say that pastors do not have a special place in the heart of God and the people, but it is when the people begin to place them before God, this contributes to the main problem. Then and only then will we be the "salt and light" that God has called us to be.

Chapter 25

And I will come near to you to judgment; and I will be a swift witness against the sorcerers, and against the adulterers, and against false swearers, and against those that oppress the hireling in his wages, the widow, and the fatherless, and that turn aside the stranger from his right, and fear not me, saith the Lord of hosts" (Malachi 3: 5).

Not all pastors are called by God. Some are called by their own greed, pride, as well as for financial gain. Here are just a few obvious traits that characterize a hireling pastor who has put himself in pastoral duty and is not chosen by God. I was searching for a final caveat to end this book and there are four tips that I found in my study (Author Unknown).

Pride

Beware of pastors who habitually refer to the congregation as "my church," instead of "the church." Acts 20:28 - Pay careful attention to yourselves and to all the flock, in which the Holy Spirit has made you overseers, to care for *the church of God*, which he obtained with his own blood.

Family

Do not trust a pastor who has children that are not model Christians themselves. Notice I did not say "perfect children." According to the Bible, if a pastor cannot take care of his own household, he cannot take care of the church. He must also love his wife as Christ loves the church. That is if he has a wife.

All called pastors do not have significant others, but are very much used in the Kingdom of God. Titus 1:6 - "Namely, if any man is above reproach, the husband of one wife, having children who believe, *not accused of rebellion*." This Scripture is simply a blue print or road map by which to follow.

Greed

Watch out for pastors who use church finances to "pay themselves" and buy extravagant homes, cars and/or other extravagant items. First Timothy 6:5 states, "And constant friction between people of corrupt mind, who have been robbed of the truth and who think that godliness is a means to financial gain."

Example

Look out for pastors who do not do as they preach, although this characteristic does not necessarily mean you should leave your church. According to Jesus in Matthew 23:3, "So you must be careful to do everything they tell you. But do not do what they do, for they do not practice what they preach. "This means as long as you are receiving the truth, even when they don't measure up to par, you should still listen to that message about the truth. You can learn something from your greatest enemy.

Having said that, make sure you do your homework! Acts 17:11 "Now the Berean Jews were of more noble character than those in Thessalonica, for they received the message with great eagerness and examined the Scriptures every day to see if what Paul said was true."

A Final Note

Do not go to a church because you are comfortable there. Plainly and simply put, choose a church that does not just teach messages on Sundays but follows and strives to be like Jesus Christ - our Lord and Savior daily.

Listen to the pastor's messages and double check if the things preached are true. The pastors are not divine, they are mortal beings that should be saved and teach salvation through our Lord and Savior Jesus Christ. Remember, they have flesh and feelings and would not be anything but empty vessels without the Holy Spirit leading them.

Do not take these signs lightly. If your pastor is arrogant, loud, and hates being corrected, then these are basic classic signs that he or she is not in line with God's Word, so where can he or she lead you?

Please note and understand that pastors are not "perfect" people. However, they should be in tune with God's Word and what God's Word requires them to do even when they mess up.

Pastors that are sent from God should understand and know how small they really are and serve the church, not control it. 1Peter 5:3 states, "Not lording over those entrusted to them, but being examples to the flock."

About the Author

Michael A. Shine was born in Birmingham, AL. to the proud parents of Mr. and Mrs. Mose Shine Jr. where he is the youngest of 7 children (five girls and two boys). He attend Kingston Elementary School, K-8 and attended Carol W. Hayes High School Class of 1989 (Birmingham, Alabama) and furthered his education at the University of Montevallo 1993, (Montevallo, Alabama) where he received a Bachelors of Business Administration Degree in Sales and Marketing and his MBA from Capella University in 2008. He also received his Juris Doctor of Law from Arizona Summit, 2009 (Phoenix, AZ) and Clerked at the Law firm of Bradley, Aarant Rose and White and his Ph.D. in Business Administration from Grand Canyon University in 2023. He is a member of Alpha Phi Alpha Fraternity, Inc.

On Father's of 1993, Michael preached his first sermon at First Baptist Church of East Boyles where he was licensed and ordained under the leadership of Rev. Clyde Beverly Sr. where he also served in the capacity of Youth Minister for 8 years. He attended Birmingham Easonian Bible College for 3 years.

He is currently a member of Face2Face Worship Center under the leadership of Lead Pastor, Anthony Xavier Page, Clinton, MD where her preaches and teaches small group Bible studies.

He currently owns his own Consulting and Legal firm (Shine's Professional Services, LLC)

He was dubbed by his family as the "Father of the Shine Family" as he carried out his father's wishes to promise to take care of the family, and to make sure holidays and special days were carried out. He stood by his father on his dying bed and made a vow to perform his eulogy and also took on the responsibility to be one of the main caretakers of his mother after the passing of his father on January 15, 2010.

In August 2012, Michael pursed his dream of publishing his first book entitled, "**Walking In Heavenly Authority**," where he was one of first African American writers to sell out his book at Barnes and Nobles Southern Writers' Showcase. The book is also now available on BN.Com, Amazon.com, and Books-A-Million .com and could purchase worldwide. He also Published a second one, entitled, "Excuse Me Pastor, I Don't Want Your Church!"

Michael's favorite movies are "The Color Purple" and "A River Ran Through it" and live by the Scripture, "1 Corinthians 13:12 - For now we see through a glass, darkly; but then face to face: now I know in part; but then shall I know even as also I am known."

To contact the author for speaking or conference engagements, send all communication to joshuaarmy11@gmail.com or via telephone at (205) 533-1707.

Bibliography

Amplified® Bible, Copyright © 1954, 1958, 1962, 1964, 1965, 1987 by The Lockman Foundation. All Rights Reserved." ()

The Holy Bible, King James Version. New York: American Bible Society: 1999; Bartleby.com, 2000.. [Date of Printout].

www.ingramcontent.com/pod-product-compliance
Lightning Source LLC
LaVergne TN
LVHW061035070526
838201LV00073B/5039